BACKYARD SONGBIRDS

An Illustrated Guide to 100 Familiar Species of North America

Marcus Schneck

Foreword by Leonard Lee Rue III

TODTRI

This book was designed and produced by
Todtri Productions Limited
254 West 31st Street
New York, NY 10001-2813
Fax: (212) 695–6984
Printed and bound in Korea

Library of Congress Catalog Card Number 91-73900

ISBN 1-57717-086-5

Author: Marcus Schneck
Publisher: Robert M. Tod
Designer and Art Director: Mark Weinberg
Editor: Mary Forsell
Typeset and Page Makeup: Strong Silent Type/NYC

TABLE OF CONTENTS

FOREWORD

The Bible talks about "the peace that passeth all understanding." I experience just such a peace each afternoon in late fall, winter and early spring by watching birds.

My home in rural northwestern New Jersey has been made into a haven for wildlife. I have many bird feeders of different kinds containing different foods. I have as many as 150 birds of fifteen to eighteen species that use these feeders continually. Each afternoon about 4 p.m., these feeders are replenished so that the birds can eat their fill and thus be fortified against the cold, dark hours ahead. After filling the feeders, I get a cup of tea and sit just inside my picture windows watching and enjoying the birds. It is my peaceful time. It is fantastic therapy. It is my way of combating the constant pressures of work and the world.

In this book, Marcus Schneck tells you how you, too, may enjoy that peace and benefit from the information he provides about the species you may see.

Mr. Schneck presents one hundred of the more common species of birds of North America that may come to, or be in the vicinity of, your feeders. The continent is broken into six zones which helps you to identify the birds you do see by listing the described birds for each zone. A photograph of each species is provided to allow for positive identification.

The "Factboxes" give a thumbnail sketch of each species by giving the most pertinent data in condensed form. I particularly like this type of presentation because the information is right to the point and can be absorbed quickly.

Valuable information is given on the types of feeders that are preferred by certain species as well as the best types of feed for each. The need for water and the proper habitat is also discovered. Mr. Schneck is well versed on this subject, being the author of "The Bird Feeder Guide."

You will enjoy this book and the birds to which it introduces you.
—Dr. Leonard Lee Rue III

INTRODUCTION

The myriad bird species that populate North America have fascinated people since Colonial times. We've lost some of those species over the more than four-century period since the first settlers arrived on the continent, and still oth-ers are endangered. Yet on the positive side of the wildlife ledger, a smaller number have actu-ally been helped by our presence here—as in the case of the American crow and mourning dove—and even by our direct intervention on their behalf—such as the eastern bluebird.

Recent decades have seen a boom in birdwatchers who not only travel coast to coast to spot and record additional bird species but also work in their backyards, on their balconies, and with any outdoor areas available to lend the birds a helping hand. These people are converting their outdoor spaces into habitats for the birds and other wildlife by focusing their attention on the three environmental aspects that every living creature needs to survive: food, water, and shelter/cover.

Food is the starting point for most of us, when we install our first birdfeeder—usually a bin-type feeder atop a pole. However, there are many other types of feeders, each with a specific purpose.

The hanging tube feeder filled with niger seeds offers a special attraction for many of our small birds, such as American goldfinches,

house finches, and purple finches. The platform or ground feeder, covered with sunflower seeds and cracked corn, is a feast for ground feeders, such as the mourning dove, blackbirds, and dark-eyed junco. Mesh bags or wire baskets stuffed with suet attract others that have no interest in seeds, such as the brown creeper and small woodpeckers. Bits of fruit are the only thing that some other species are looking for, such as the orioles.

In addition to maintaining the widest possible variety in types of feeders, try keeping them stocked year-round. You will no doubt be amazed by the additional bird activity, particularly during courting and nesting periods, that this will permit you to view.

Water is the habitat element that has been most neglected in the past. It is also the single most important thing that backyard owners can do to enhance their habitat offerings. Many

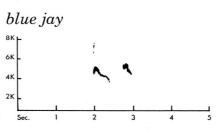

blue jay

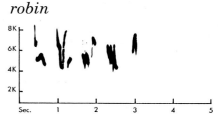

robin

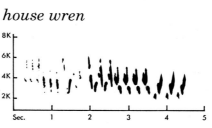

house wren

The above "Real Time" sonograms, or sound spectrograms, illustrate the typical songs of the blue jay, robin and house wren. The frequency markers are at 1-kHZ intervals, the time marker in seconds.

species that generally won't visit feeders both need and relish water for drinking and baths.

The sound of running or dripping water is a further attraction to most species. You may wish to suspend a dripping hose or jug with a tiny hole above the birdbath. On a more elaborate level, it might mean adding a waterfall or fountain to an in-ground minipond.

If you can maintain a small patch of open dirt in your backyard, many species will reward the effort by taking regular dust baths there.

Shelter/cover protects birds, their nests, and their young from both their enemies and the elements, such as wind, rain, and snow. Trees, shrubs, wildflowers, weeds, and even grasses perform this function. Each bird species has its own special preference, which you will read about under individual bird entries.

Touch all of these bases in one way or another and, no matter how small your outside area may be, you will bring many new species into that space for your viewing and learning pleasure.

HOW TO USE THIS BOOK

The following pages are designed for use in two very different ways. The 100 Factboxes accompanying each species description allow for easy identification of the most common backyard songbirds of North America. To make quick identifications when you see a new bird species, first page swiftly through the first chapter, "Pancontinental Birds," and scan the photos in the Factboxes. These are some of the most widespread and common birds to be found virtually everywhere on the continent, with some localized exceptions.

If you don't find the bird pictured there, turn next to the chapter of the book that covers your region. Page quickly through this section, again scanning the photos in the Factboxes. This same procedure can be followed if you come across the nest and/or eggs of a new bird species. Each Factbox includes descriptions of both of these important aspects for that species.

Finally, if you still have not located the bird, turn to the last few paragraphs of the chapter

for your region. There you will find references to birds in other chapters of the book that also are to be found in your region.

It is possible that you will not find the bird in question in this book. There are a vast number of species, approximately 645 breeding species, inhabiting various regions of North America, and we've chosen 100 of the most common songbirds and arranged them by region. In this manner, we hope to help the reader discover those birds most likely to be found in and near the backyard.

Of course, there are many other species that could have been included in these pages. For example, we've listed 50 other such species. But

and fall is one reason for such movement. Food supply is another: In some instances food scarcity drives birds into new and different settings, while some species have such wide-ranging appetites that they can make their home under many different circumstances.

Therefore, some species included in this book are likely to be residents of your neighborhood throughout the year; others generally prefer woodland or swamp habitats, but during migration are likely to appear in backyards and parks.

Aside from identifying songbirds, another important use for this book is to attract desired species into your backyard. The text that follows offers insights into the habitat and food preferences of the birds. There is also a listing of food preferences at the back of the book. To attract a specific species, if it occurs in your region, duplicate what you read here in your backyard and you'll greatly increase your chances.

working within our space limitations, and still wanting to supply enough information about each species covered to make the book a useful reference, we've tried to select those birds that you are likely to see and hear.

Birds travel greater distances than most other species of wildlife, and for this reason they are found at different times in a great many regions of the continent and in a great many different habitats. Migration each spring

FACTBOX ABBREVIATIONS

For ease of description under the "Range" category, we have divided the U.S. and Canada each into three zones, running east-west across the countries. Then, there are six horizontal zones to the North American continent: northern Canada, central Canada, southern Canada, northern U.S., central U.S., and southern U.S.

Other regions: Many of the birds described in this book are common in more than one region, while still not occurring throughout all of the U.S. and southern Canada. For these birds, we've added this "other regions" listing, which lists the regions where it occurs in addition to the one where we've listed it. The abbreviations are: NE, Northeast and Mid-Atlantic; SE, Southeast; PP, Plains & Prairies; SW, Southwest; RM, Rockies; PC, Pacific Coast; and SC, Southern Canada.

1.
Pancontinental Birds

MOURNING DOVE
Zenaida macroura
Family: Columbidae
Description: 12"; sand gray throughout with black wing bars and white borders on tail.
Habitat: Open areas—agricultural to residential—with scattered trees.
Range: Breeds from southern Canada south to Gulf of Mexico; winters south of the U.S.-Canadian border.
Nest: Twigs in loose mass in shrub or tree.
Eggs: White; 2 to 3 per clutch.
Song: "Coo-ah, cooo, cooo, cooo" (rolling, twirling).

HORNED LARK
Eremophila alpestris
Family: Alaudidae
Description: 7 to 8"; brown throughout with black crescent across breast, black line under each eye and black "horns," which may not always be visible.
Habitat: Areas with thick grassy and weedy covering.
Range: Breeds central Canada south to Gulf of Mexico, except for the Deep South; winters southern Canada south to Gulf of Mexico.
Nest: Depression in ground lined with soft plant fibers.
Eggs: Gray spotted with brown; 3 to 5 per clutch.
Song: "Ti-ti."
Call: Series of tinkling notes, while in flight.

MOURNING DOVE

Common in all parts of the U.S. and many parts of southern Canada, the mourning dove is another of the species that has benefited by European settlement of North America. As settlers cleared away the forest to build homesteads, the open habitat needed by the dove was maximized and the amazingly reproductive bird quickly filled the niche with its numbers.

In some states, the mourning dove is protected as a songbird. In others, it is hunted as a gamebird. Regardless, the bird is one of our most common backyard visitors. A ground feeder filled with cracked corn will bring the local mourning doves into a pattern of visits several times each day, but particularly at early morning and late afternoon.

HORNED LARK

The horned lark is one of North America's earliest nesting species. Nests are regularly discovered as early as February, and it is not uncommon for a pair's first clutch to be destroyed in late winter storms.

Short grassy areas are the preferred habitat for the horned lark, which generally abandons a site as soon as an appreciable amount of vegetation takes hold.

In the fall, large flocks of horned larks, pipits, buntings, and longspurs swarm over residential areas.

AMERICAN CROW

The American crow is one species that actually has benefited from the coming to North America of the early settlers. There are many more of this species today than there were when Columbus landed on this side of the Atlantic. In some areas, crows gather in rookeries of 500,000-plus birds.

A half-dozen or less is a much more common sight in the backyard, where pieces of bread and other food scraps spread on the lawn will attract regular visits by the same group of birds at about the same time each day.

Crows are inclined to steal and hide bright objects that are small enough for them to grasp in their strong beaks. Buttons, marbles, bits of tin foil, polished stones, and the like are among their favorites. They will readily make off with any such items placed in the backyard.

HOUSE WREN

When a small mass of twigs and feathers shows up in the pocket of a coat hanging on the clothesline, you can be relatively certain that a pair of house wrens has set up housekeeping in your neighborhood. The common little bird has built a solid reputation for nesting in many odd places in close proximity to people, including flower pots, door wreaths, and mailboxes.

They also readily accept small nesting boxes, which are among the best means for attracting the birds. The decision on whether to try to bring them into the backyard must be tempered with the fact that the house wrens often attacks and cracks the eggs of other birds nesting within its chosen territory.

Remarkably, the house wren is generally a shy, retiring bird, often difficult to observe, when not in the breeding mode.

Almost all small birds build a new nest each spring, even when the nest from the previous year is still intact and exactly where the birds built it. They have been observed dismantling the old nest and then rebuilding in the same location with some of the same materials they just tore apart.

AMERICAN CROW
Corvus brachychynchos
Family: Corvidae
Description: 17 to 21"; black throughout, including large bill and shining eyes; very stocky with fanned tail.
Habitat: Residential, agricultural, and woodland areas.
Range: Breeds from central Canada south to Gulf of Mexico; winters from southern Canada south to Gulf of Mexico.
Nest: Twigs in loose tangle lined with plant fibers, grass, feathers, and other small materials, in very high crotch of tree.
Eggs: Bluish green spotted with brown and gray; 4 to 6 per clutch.
Song: "Caw-caw-caw."
Call: Rattles and clicks.

HOUSE WREN
Troglodytes aedon
Family: Troglodytidae
Description: 4½ to 5¼"; dull brown, paler below, very short tail.
Habitat: Agricultural and residential areas, also along edges of woodlands.
Range: Breeds from central Canada south to Gulf of Mexico and through northern Mexico; breeds as far north as southern California and South Carolina.
Nest: Twigs stuffed into cavity and lined with plant fibers, feathers, and similarly soft materials.
Eggs: White spotted with brown; 5 to 8 per clutch.
Song: Bubbling twitter, rising and falling.
Call: Angry chatter.

AMERICAN ROBIN

The American robin is generally viewed as a harbinger of spring. But this member of the thrush family actually winters in considerable numbers in the thick forests and swamps in the northern states. Others do migrate north and south and it is these that generally are noted as the "first robin of spring" on their annual return.

A large lawn that has not been treated with chemicals, and thus generally holds a healthy population of earthworms (a large portion of the bird's diet), is the key to attracting this species. Birdbaths and dirt areas for dust baths also are prime attractions.

NORTHERN MOCKINGBIRD

Although the northern mockingbird can become an aggressive bully in any backyard that it claims within its territory, its magical habit of mimicking other birds, other animals, and even mechanical sounds makes it a welcome addition for most bird enthusiasts. Individual northern mockingbirds have been documented as rendering the sounds of more than three dozen other bird species. Sometimes, irritatingly, the bird will choose to let loose it repertoire for several hours during the middle of the night.

The species is largely a fruit eater, and berry-producing shrubs—particularly with heavy thorns and tangled branches—are the primary means of bringing them into the backyard and holding them there.

The average backyard will hold a solitary northern mockingbird during much of the year. But, if the habitat and food supply are adequate, that number will jump to two as the breeding season approaches and then to three or four as the fledglings leave the nest. Soon thereafter there will be much chasing and fighting, as the previous "hermit" works to drive all the others from its territory.

AMERICAN ROBIN
Turdus migratorius
Family: Turdidae
Description: 9 to 11"; dusky gray above, dirty orange-red below; male has black head and tail; female replaces black with dusky gray.
Habitat: Residential, agricultural, and open woodland areas.
Range: Breeds from central Canada south to Gulf of Mexico, but only rarely in the Deep South; winters from southernmost Canada south throughout the U.S.
Nest: Small twigs and grass cemented with mud into a cup lined with softer plant fibers, in the fork of a tree or on a ledge of any sort.
Eggs: "Robin's-egg-blue" eggs; 3 to 5 per clutch.
Song: "Cheer-up, cheerily, cheer-up, cheerily."
Call: "Tut-tut-tut."

NORTHERN MOCKINGBIRD
Mimus polyglottos
Family: Mimidae
Description: 9 to 11"; gray with bright white patches on wings and tail, long gray tail.
Habitat: Areas with thickets and hedgerows, from agricultural lands to backyards to brushland in the desert.
Range: Breeds from southern Canada south to Gulf of Mexico; winters in the southern two-thirds of the U.S.
Nest: Twigs and heavy plant fibers loosely woven into cup, in thick shrub, hedge, or low tree.
Eggs: Blue-green blotched with brown; 3 to 5 per clutch.
Song: Widely varying and lengthy series of musical notes and harsh cries, each repeated three or more times; often imitates the sounds of other birds and other creatures.
Call: "Tchak."

CEDAR WAXWING
Bombycilla cedrorum
Family: Bombycillidae
Description: 6½ to 8"; brown throughout with black face, shiny red tips on wing feathers, yellow tips on tail; both sexes have brown crest.
Habitat: Wooded areas with minimal undergrowth, such as orchards and backyards with ample shade trees.
Range: Breeds from central Canada south to Georgia and California; winters from New England in the East and southern Canada in the West south to Panama.
Nest: Twigs and grass loosely woven into cup, in fork or branch fork of tree.
Eggs: Grayish blue spotted with brown and black; 4 to 6 per clutch.
Song: "Zeee, zeee" (buzzingly).

CEDAR WAXWING

Berries are the key to attracting the cedar waxwing. Even the bird's late summer nesting period is timed to coincide with the heaviest berry crops of the year. The young are fed a diet with higher fruit content than those of most other species, although summer insects also are taken on the wing.

Cedar waxwings often are seen in flocks of a few hundred that will suddenly come onto the scene when a berry crop matures only to vanish a few days later when the crop is depleted. For this reason they can be the scourge of fruit farmers.

Their social habits include some peculiar customs, such as passing fruits from one bird to the next throughout a long line sitting on the same tree limb or wire. Eventually one of the birds—and not always the last in the row—will gulp down the tidbit, causing the whole process to begin again.

LOGGERHEAD SHRIKE

The loggerhead shrike is relatively unique among songbirds for its predatory habits against small birds and rodents. The bird sits motionless on a perch that offers a commanding view, waiting for another species of bird or a mouse to appear. It may also hover in the air, waiting for the same opportunity. When the prey appears, the shrike drops onto it.

Lacking the talons of a hawk, the shrike kills its prey with its beak. It then impales its prey on a barbed wire fence or large thorn, which holds it in place for rending into bite-size bits. This habit has given the shrike its other common name of butcher bird.

WARBLING VIREO

A backyard filled with mature shade trees and bordering on a stream is the most likely residential area to attract the warbling vireo. It spends most of its time in the tops of the trees, searching for insects to eat.

Elms are the preferred tree of this vireo and the Dutch elm disease which has decimated this tree species over the past century has in turn reduced the bird's population. Nevertheless, it is still common in many locales.

YELLOW WARBLER

The yellow warbler occupies the widest range of any warbler species in North America. As such, the bird varies widely across its range, both in appearance and habits. However, wherever it occurs, the yellow warbler's diet is made up mostly of some of the most harmful insects, such as borers, aphids, and grasshoppers.

It is a primary target of the cowbird, which has the habit of leaving its eggs in the nests of other species for hatching and care by the foster parents. The yellow warbler responds by building a new bottom to its nest, right over the offending egg, as well as any of its own that have already been laid. Nests of five and six layers have been discovered.

WARBLING VIREO
Vireo gilvus
Family: Vireonidae
Description: 5 to 6"; olive green above, off-white below, white eyebrow.
Habitat: Woodlands of deciduous trees, especially near wet areas, also shade trees.
Range: Breeds from central Canada south to Gulf of Mexico; winters in Central America.
Nest: Plants fibers and bits of barks woven into cup and attached to forked branch near top of tall tree.
Eggs: White lightly spotted with brown and black; 3 to 5 per clutch.
Song: Sleepy warbling, similar to purple finch but slower and rising at end.
Call: "Tway-tway."

YELLOW WARBLER
Dendroica petechia
Family: Parulidae
Description: 4½ to 5"; yellow throughout except yellowish olive on back, male also sho red-brown streaks on breast and brighter yello spots on tail.
Habitat: Thick brush in moist areas, such as along streams and swamps; also in residential areas.
Range: Breeds from Alaska and central Cand da south to South America; winters north as fo as southern Mexico.
Nest: Plant fibers and bits of bark woven into cup, in small tree.
Eggs: Pale bluish white blotched with brown and gray; 4 to 5 per clutch.
Song: "Sweet-sweet-sweet, little-more-sweet."

COMMON YELLOWTHROAT

For most of the year, the common yellowthroat is a shy and retiring bird, spending its time in the thick weeds of the marsh. But during the spring breeding season, the male performs one of the most showy courtship flight displays of any North American bird. It launches itself into the air, emitting a mishmash of high-pitched notes, then falls back to the ground and sings its normal song of "witchity-witchity-witchity-witchity."

Although no formal investigation has been mounted into the feeding habits of the common yellowthroat, recorded observations reflect a diet composed almost entirely of a variety of insects. Habitat appears to be the primary means of bringing the species into the backyard.

YELLOW-BREASTED CHAT

The display flight of the male yellow-breasted chat offers a comical sight for the spring birdwatcher. Fluttering up into the air a short way and then falling back to earth, again and again, the would-be mate allows its legs to hang limply under its body. All the while it sings courtship notes.

A wide variety of insects make up the bulk of the chat's diet, although it shows a real fondness for berries, both wild and domestic. Feeders must contain some fruit to attract this species.

COMMON YELLOWTHROAT

Geothlypis trichas
Family: Parulidae
Description: 4½ to 6"; olive above, lemon yellow on throat and breast; male has black face.
Habitat: Damp areas with heavy brush.
Range: Breeds Alaska and central Canada south to Gulf of Mexico; winters north to central California and Virginia.
Nest: Grasses, bits of bark and sedges woven loosely and lined with hair and fine plant fibers, on or near ground in weeds.
Eggs: White spotted with dark brown and gray; 3 to 5 per clutch.
Song: "Witchity-witchity-witchity-witchity."
Call: "Tchep."

YELLOW-BREASTED CHAT

Icteria virens
Family: Parulidae
Description: 6½ to 7½"; olive green with yellow breast, white rump and eye rings, black bill and face.
Habitat: Thick brush along streams and on dry hillsides.
Range: Breeds from southern Canada south to Gulf of Mexico and into northern Mexico; winters Central America north to Mexico.
Nest: Grass, leaves, and bits of bark in large bundle lined with smaller grasses, in thick shrub.
Eggs: White spotted with brown; 4 to 5 per clutch.
Song: Series of croaks and whistles.

RUFOUS-SIDED TOWHEE

Primarily a species of woodland thickets and edges, the rufous-sided towhee nevertheless makes more than enough appearances in residential areas to warrant membership in our group of backyard songbirds. Even on these visits to man's haunts, it favors those backyards that offer thick hedgerows with layers of dead leaves beneath them. It scratches through these leaves in search of insects.

The wonderful markings of the male—although actually nothing more than shades of black, white, and brown—constitute a justifiable excuse for property owners to tend to their leaf-raking chores just a bit less earnestly.

CHIPPING SPARROW

The chipping sparrow has adapted well to human inhabitation of North America. Originally a resident of forest clearings and edges, the small singer now makes it home quite readily in the backyards and parks of our suburban areas.

Likewise, it has adapted to the changing times in its choice of nesting materials. Originally, the hair of wild animals made up a substantial portion of the lining of its nest. When the horse became a common fixture on the American landscape, that animal accordingly become a prime source of nest lining. Now that the horse has all but vanished from many areas with the reduction of farming, the chipping sparrow makes do with human and pet hair, as well as any wild animal hair it encounters.

RUFOUS-SIDED TOWHEE
Pipilo erythrophthalmus
Family: Fringillidae
Description: 7 to 9½"; male has white belly, black back and on head, and namesake rufous in flank areas; female is similar but with brown in place of black.
Habitat: Brushy areas along edges of woodlands.
Range: Breeds from southern Canada to Gulf of Mexico; winters north to northern U.S. in East and southernmost Canada in West.
Nest: Plant fibers, bits of bark and grass in a cup, in thick weeds on ground or very close to ground.
Eggs: Grayish white spotted with reddish brown; 3 to 6 per clutch.
Song: "Drink-your-teeeee" (gaily).
Call: "Tow-weeee" (loudly).

CHIPPING SPARROW
Spizella passerina
Family: Fringillidae
Description: 5 to 5¾"; streaked with various shades of brown and black above, gray below, red-brown crown with gray on face and white eyebrow, gray on rump.
Habitat: Grassy, weedy spots in residential areas, pastures, and near woodlands.
Range: Breeds from northern Canada south to southern U.S.; winters north as far as northern California in the West and Pennsylvania in the East.
Nest: Grass and plant fibers woven into cup and lined with hair, in shrubs or amid vines.
Eggs: Pale bluish green spotted and scrawled with dark brown; 3 to 5 per clutch.
Song: Light, swift trill.

VESPER SPARROW

Poecetes gramineus
Family: Fringillidae
Description: 5 to 6½"; streaked with gray-brown, white at outside of tail feathers and around eye, red-brown at "elbows" of wings.
Habitat: Grassy areas in agricultural and residential zones.
Range: Breeds central Canada south to Gulf of Mexico, except for the Deep South; winters south of the U.S.-Canadian border to Gulf of Mexico.
Nest: Grass and small roots woven into cup, among weeds and grass on ground.
Eggs: Creamy white spotted with brown and gray; 3 to 6 per clutch.
Song: "Come-come-where-where-all-together-down-the-hill."

VESPER SPARROW

The name of the vesper sparrow is the legacy of one man's impressions about the bird. Naturalist John Burroughs, who discovered the small bird, felt that its wonderful song was further enhanced by the evening air. Whether in accord with his impression or not, many agree that the vesper sparrow's song lends a distinctive air to agricultural areas.

The vesper sparrow spends a great deal of time on the ground, in areas of low grass, where it prefers to run ahead of any threat until pressed very closely. Dust baths are a favorite, daily activity, engaged in frequently and with relish.

SONG SPARROW

A wide variety of potentially harmful insects, from grasshoppers to beetles, make up about half of the song sparrow's diet during the summer months. The rest of the year the bird turns to seeds of many different weeds and domestic plants. A regular feeder visitor, the song sparrow generally defines its winter territory by available feeders.

Some of the species' other names, such as everybody's darling and silver tongue, attest to the wonderful melody of its song.

SONG SPARROW

Melospiza melodia
Family: Fringillidae
Description: 5 to 7"; streaked in various shades of brown with large brown spot at center of breast; flicks tail while in flight.
Habitat: Brushy and weedy areas in agricultural and residential zones.
Range: Breeds from Alaska and central Canada south to Gulf of Mexico; winter from southern Canada south to Gulf of Mexico.
Nest: Grass and leaves woven into cup and lined with hair, in weedy areas on ground or in low shrub.
Eggs: Greenish white spotted with red-brown and purple; 3 to 5 per clutch.
Song: "Made-made-made, put-on-your-tea-kettle-kettle-kettle."

DARK-EYED JUNCO

It's likely that you know the dark-eyed junco by a different, local name, such as showbird, than the generally accepted common name for the species. The bird occurs in many geographical variations across the continent, and previously many of these variations were considered to be entirely separate species. However, interbreeding is common wherever the different "species" come into contact, and thus we see that they are all the same type.

Whatever you call the dark-eyed junco, it's likely that it is one of your most common birds at your winter feeders. However, it prefers to feed on the ground and is often content to snatch up the seeds that other birds knock from the feeders. Oil-type sunflower seeds are a favorite.

DARK-EYED JUNCO

Junco hyemalis
Family: Fringillidae
Description: 5½ to 6½"; gray to gray-brown above, lighter gray on breast, white on abdomen and at sides of tail, pink bill.
Habitat: Forest of coniferous or mixed species; also in residential areas in winter.
Range: Breeds from Alaska and central Canada south in mountain regions to Georgia in the East and Mexico in the West; winters south to Gulf of Mexico and into Mexico.
Nest: Grass, bits of bark and grass woven into cup, in grass and weed on or very close to the ground.
Eggs: Pale bluish white spotted and blotched with brown and purple; 3 to 5 per clutch.
Song: Trill similar to chipping sparrow although slower.
Call: Series of clicking notes.

31

RED-WINGED BLACKBIRD
Agelaius phoeniceus
Family: Icteridae
Description: 7 to 9½"; male coal black with crimson patches on shoulders; female streaked in various shades of dull brown. Looks like large sparrow.
Habitat: Wet and damp areas from swamps to pastures.
Range: Breeds from Alaska and northern Canada south to Gulf of Mexico; winters as far north as Pennsylvania in the East and southernmost Canada in the West.
Nest: Grass and other vegetation woven into cup, attached to tall stalk of various types of wetland vegetation or limb of small shrub.
Eggs: Pale greenish blue spotted, streaked and blotched with dark brown and red-brown; 3 to 5 per clutch.
Song: "O-ka-reeee"; also "tse-er, tse-er."

RED-WINGED BLACKBIRD

More often a resident of wet places, such as swamps and marshes, the red-winged blackbird nonetheless ventures frequently into backyards that are relatively close to such natural landscapes. Feeding periods, most often occurring during midmorning to midafternoon, concentrate the birds on areas adjacent to those wet places.

Weed seeds and grain make up about three-quarters of the bird's diet year-round, even more during the winter months, when insects are harder to come by. Where the red-winged blackbird winters, flocks will become regular visitors to feeders stocked with grains, cracked corn, and breadcrumbs.

NORTHERN ORIOLE

Formerly called the Baltimore oriole in the East and Bullock's oriole in the West, the northern oriole is known today as a single species. This realization was helped along by human planting of trees through the Great Plains. The newly wooded areas allowed the two groups to connect and the subsequent interbreeding proved that they were actually races of the same species.

The nest of the northern oriole—a hanging basket of soft plant fibers, string, and the like—is recognizable to even the newest birdwatcher. To construct this amazing design, the bird readily accepts bits of yarn placed out in the backyard.

Fruit is an effective attraction. Segments of citrus fruit hung from tree limbs or placed on small skewers are key to bringing the species into the backyard. The oriole also readily drinks from hummingbird feeders.

NORTHERN ORIOLE
Icterus galbula
Family: Icteridae
Description: 7 to 8½"; male orange on breast, shoulder, and rump, black on head, wings and tail; female olive-brown above, dull orange and white below, dull white wing bars.
Habitat: Woodlands of primarily deciduous species, also residential areas with mature shade trees.
Range: Breeds from central Canada south throughout most of the U.S., as far west as the Great Plains; winters in Central and South America.
Nest: Strips of bark, plant fibers, string, and similar materials woven into bag, hanging from tree limb.
Eggs: Pale grayish white spotted and scrawled with brown and black; 4 to 6 per clutch.
Song: Single or double flutelike notes whistled quickly.
Call: Harsh rattle.

HOUSE FINCH

One of the more common backyard species throughout much of North America, the house finch is a prime example of how an introduced species can flourish in new surroundings. Until the 1940s, the house finch was found east only as far as Texas and Nebraska. But an aborted attempt at making it a cagebird in New York City resulted in the release into the wild of a few pairs. The species is now well established throughout much of the East as well.

Because of its relatively new status in the wild in the East, the species relies very heavily on feeders, particularly those filled with niger or oil-type sunflower seeds. Flocks of the small reddish birds will return again and again throughout the spring, summer, and fall to feeders that they frequented during the winter, even when those feeders are no longer filled with seeds.

HOUSE FINCH

Carpodacus mexicanus
Family: Fringillidae
Description: 5 to 6"; male mostly streaked brown with deep red head, breast, and rump; female streaked brown throughout.
Habitat: In close proximity to man; also in brushy areas of deserts in the West.
Range: Southern Canada and south.
Nest: Twigs and grass woven into a cup, in a shrub or cavity.
Eggs: Pale bluish green spotted with black; 4 to 5 per clutch.
Song: Clear burry warble, similar to purple finch but weaker.
Call: "Cheap."

PINE SISKIN

Some winters, large flocks of pine siskins can be seen at feeders across the U.S. In other years, very few of the birds will wander below the U.S.-Canadian border. It all depends on the seed crop of any given year in the forests of northern Canada. If the crop fails, the U.S. will have an excellent year of pine siskins at backyard feeders.

Salt holds a special attraction for the pine siskin. Flocks gather along highways in the winter, gleaning what they can from the salt that was spread to melt ice. Small salt blocks or sheltered plates of salt will help to bring them into the backyard.

AMERICAN GOLDFINCH

Its other common name—wild canary—attests to the wonderful, lemon-yellow and black coloration of the male American goldfinch during the breeding season. It is one of North America's most colorful birds and is common in backyards across the continent.

Seeds are by far the primary food of the goldfinch; this bird even delays it nesting until mid to late summer so that wildflower seed crops are readily available. The much-hated thistle is a prime source of seeds for this species, while the thistle's down is used in the construction of its nest. Niger seeds in a hanging tube feeder will hold a flock—possibly mixed with redpolls and siskins—to a small area throughout the year. However, the winter flock generally will be noticeably larger than the summer grouping.

PINE SISKIN
Carduelis pinus
Family: Fringillidae
Description: 4½ to 5¼"; streaked in various shades of brown with small patches of yellow on wings and tail, notched tail.
Habitat: Woodlands of coniferous or coniferous and deciduous trees; grasslands with brush and thickets.
Range: Breeds from Alaska and mid-Canada south into northernmost U.S. in the East and almost to Mexico in the West; winters throughout that range and south to Gulf of Mexico.
Nest: Twigs, bits of bark and moss lined with plant fibers, hair and feathers, in a coniferous tree.
Eggs: Pale greenish blue spotted with dark brown; 2 to 6 per clutch.
Song: "Bzzzzzt" (ascending).

AMERICAN GOLDFINCH
Carduelis tristis
Family: Fringillidae
Description: 4½ to 5½"; male in breeding plumage has lemon yellow coloration with black forehead, black with white edges on wings and tail, and white rump; female and male in winter are grayish olive with duller black and white markings.
Habitat: Brushy and weedy areas with thickets and grasslands near trees.
Range: Breeds throughout southern Canada and the northern two-thirds of the U.S.; winters from southern Canada to Gulf of Mexico and southern Mexico.
Nest: Grass and plant fibers woven into a cup lined with thistle and cattail down, in the fork of a low shrub or small tree.
Eggs: Pale blue-white; 4 to 6 per clutch.
Song: Series of short trills and twitters.
Call: "Per-chick-o-ree" (while in flight).

BLUE JAY
Cyanocitta cristata
Family: Corvidae
Description: 12"; deep blue above, white below, white and black markings on face, wings, and tail, strong crest.
Habitat: Wooded areas, parks, and backyards, especially where oak trees abound.
Range: East of Rockies from southern Canada to Gulf of Mexico.
Nest: Loosely woven twigs lined with plant fibers, in the fork of a tree.
Eggs: Greenish brown blotched with brown; 3 to 6 per clutch.
Song: Variety of calls, including harsh "jaay-jaay," purring "queedle-queedle," and the "kee-yeeer" scream of the red-shouldered hawk.
Other regions: Also SE, PP, SW, and SC.

BLUE JAY

Some backyard birdwatchers are not particularly fond of the blue jay because of its habit of taking over the birdfeeder and chasing smaller birds from the seeds. However, the jay's behavior really is rather short-lived, lasting only until the birds—blue jays usually travel in small groups—have carried off their fill of seeds. In exchange, they fill the landscape with bright flurries of blue and provide quite a bit of action.

Peanuts in the shell are a particular attraction for the blue jay, which will leave all other seeds untouched so long as the nuts are available to be carried off, one by one.

Blue jays are seen throughout the year across their range, but the birds of summer often are different birds than those in winter. The species is migratory, with birds from farther north replacing their southern counterparts as the entire population shifts southward in the fall.

BLACK-CAPPED CHICKADEE
Parus atricapillus
Family: Paridae
Description: 4¾ to 5¾"; gray above, off-white below, black cap and throat, white cheeks, faint white edge on wing feathers.
Habitat: Open woodlands of deciduous and mixed species; also, suburban areas in winter.
Range: Breeds from Alaska and central Canada south through the northern third of the U.S.; winters south as far as Maryland and Texas.
Nest: Plant fibers, moss, grass, fur, and feathers woven into cup in cavity.
Eggs: White spotted with red-brown; 5 to 10 per clutch.
Call: "Chick-a-dee-dee-dee;" also, whistles "fee-bee."
Other regions: PP, RM, PC, and SC.

BLACK-CAPPED CHICKADEE
One of the most gregarious and curious backyard birds, the black-capped chickadee can be tamed to the point that it will take seeds from your hand. To do this, scatter oil-type sunflower seeds around the spot where you will later do the hand-feeding. Allow the chickadees to feed on these seeds for a few days, then sit down in the middle of the area and remain very still. Fill your cupped hand with seeds and hold it out away from your body, in a position that is comfortable enough for you to remain still for some time. In just a few attempts, you should have one or more of the birds eating out of your hands.

Black-capped chickadees are often seen in mixed flocks with nuthatches, small woodpeckers, titmice, creepers, and kinglets, traveling through the winter landscape from feeder to feeder. These flocks generally appear at the same feeders at about the same time each day.

39

TUFTED TITMOUSE
Parus bicolor
Family: Paridae
Description: 5 to 6"; gray above, white below, red-brown sides, gray crest.
Habitat: Damp, wooded areas; in winter, more suburban than at other times of year.
Range: From the U.S.-Canadian border south to Gulf of Mexico, in the eastern half of the U.S.
Nest: Mass of leaves and moss stuffed into cavity.
Eggs: White spotted with light brown; 4 to 8 per clutch.
Song: "Here-a, here-a, here-a."
Call: "Peter-Peter" (repeated many times in whistling tone).
Other regions: SE and PP (eastern).

TUFTED TITMOUSE

Tufted titmice will also appear in the same mixed flocks with chickadees. As most of the different species in these groups feed while hanging on the sides of tree trunks, suspended mesh bags of suet or wire cages of suet attached to tree trunks or feeder poles are strong attractions for them during the cold months.

They also relish oil-type sunflower seeds, taking them one by one for storage in bark crevices in nearby tree trunks.

The tufted titmouse prefers an environment of swamps and marshes, but has adapted well to suburban developments and city parks, so long as they offer ample deciduous trees. The bird shows little fear of humans, even to the extent of following its curiosity to come closer at the sound of the human voice.

RED-BREASTED NUTHATCH

The primary winter food of the red-breasted nuthatch is the seed of coniferous trees in its northern breeding grounds, but when the crop of those trees fails large numbers of the birds will migrate southward. At these times, the birds are regular visitors to backyard feeders—although not as frequent as their white-breasted cousins—and chopped nuts and suet are primary attractions.

While feeding, the red-breasted nuthatch will make repeated trips from the source of the food to the trunk of a nearby tree. It will carry one seed or one nut on each trip, jam it into the cracks in the barks, and crack it open with its bill. It is another of the species that can be tamed to take seed from human hands.

RED-BREASTED NUTHATCH
Sitta canadensis
Family: Sittidae
Description: 4½ to 4¾"; bluish gray above, red-brown below and on crown, white eyebrow.
Habitat: Coniferous woodlands, although more diverse during migration.
Range: Breeds from Alaska and central Canada south to central U.S.; winters in southern U.S. and northern Mexico.
Nest: Twigs and grass woven into cup and lined with plant fibers, in cavity; edges of entrance hole "painted" with pine pitch.
Eggs: White spotted with red-brown; 4 to 7 per clutch.
Call: "Yank-yank" (higher in pitch than white-breasted nuthatch).
Other regions: SE, PP, RM, PC, and SC.

WHITE-BREASTED NUTHATCH

Larger and more stay-at-home than the red-breasted nuthatch, the pairs of white-breasted nuthatch in the neighborhood quickly become regulars at feeders, as soon as they are filled with seeds in the fall.

Pairs of white-breasted nuthatches remain together throughout the year, but they will join with the roaming mixed flocks of chickadees, creepers, small woodpeckers, and kinglets while those mixed flocks are within the nuthatches' territory.

WHITE-BREASTED NUTHATCH
Sitta carolinensis
Family: Sittidae
Description: 5 to 6"; bluish gray above, white below and on face, black crown.
Habitat: Woodlands of deciduous and mixed species.
Range: Southern Canada south to Gulf of Mexico and Mexico.
Nest: Twigs and grass woven into cup lined with hair and feathers, in cavity.
Eggs: White spotted with brown and lavender; 5 to 10 per clutch.
Song: "Whi-whi-whi-whi-whi" (rapidly).
Call: "Yank-yank" (lower in pitch than the red-breasted nuthatch).
Other regions: SE, PP (eastern), SW, RM, PC, and SC (southernmost).

BROWN CREEPER

Certhia americana
Family: Certhiidae
Description: 5 to 6"; streaked brown throughout, erect tail.
Habitat: Woodlands of deciduous and mixed species.
Range: Alaska and central Canada south to Gulf of Mexico.
Nest: Twigs, bits of bark, moss, and feathers woven into loose cup against trunk of tree.
Eggs: White spotted with brown; 6 to 7 per clutch.
Song: Descending warble.
Call: "Tsee."
Other regions: SE, PP, RM, PC, and SC.

BROWN CREEPER

The small brown bird spiraling its way up around the trunk of the tree in the background often goes unnoticed as its more flamboyant traveling companions—chickadees, small woodpeckers, nuthatches, and kinglets—occupy center stage. But, if you look closely when these mixed flocks enter the backyard in winter, chances are good that you'll spot the brown creepers.

While the more familiar nuthatches generally travel headfirst down tree trunks, the brown creeper moves *up* the trunk. As it reaches the highest point that it chooses to mount in its search for insects hidden in bark, the bird flits down to the base of another tree and begins its ascent again.

EASTERN BLUEBIRD

A symbol of the impact that backyard birding activities can have on bird populations, the eastern bluebird has been brought back from the edge of extinction by human intervention. As settlers developed North America, the bird's habitat of hedgerows and nesting cavities was lost as more efficient farming techniques and growing housing developments changed our approach to the land. In addition, two species that Europeans introduced to the continent—house sparrows and European starlings—successfully competed with the bluebird for the nesting cavities that remained.

By 1963, annual counts of birds across the continent determined that the eastern bluebird population then stood at just ten percent of what it had been before the advent of European immigration to North America.

As a result of the 1963 count, concerned people began to take action on behalf of the bluebirds. Individuals and groups organized to save the bluebird erected manmade nesting boxes to replace the lost natural nesting cavities in trees and fence posts. The bird's decline has been reversed by these efforts.

EASTERN BLUEBIRD
Sialia sialis
Family: Turdidae
Description: 6½ to 7½"; bright blue above, red-brown breast, white belly; female duller than male.
Habitat: Open grassy, weedy areas with scattered trees.
Range: Breeds from southern Canada south to Gulf of Mexico and into the mountains of Mexico, east of the Rockies; winters from Virginia south through Gulf of Mexico and into Mexico.
Nest: Grasses and other plant fibers wove into loose cup, in a cavity.
Eggs: Light blue; 3 to 6 per clutch.
Song: Warble interrupted occasionally with chattering note.
Call: "Queedle" (flowing, while in flight).
Other regions: SE, PP, and SC.

PINE WARBLER

Only in its migration flight is the pine warbler found outside of its natural habitat of pine forests. At these times it can be observed in parks and backyards dominated by deciduous trees and shrubs. At all other times, including the breeding season, pine trees—the more, the better—are the key factor in attracting the small bird.

It eats a wide assortment of insects and spiders and, when they are unavailable, seeds from various shrubs, weeds, and grasses. Feeder visits can be encouraged with a mixture of half peanut butter and half moistened corn meal. Suet feeders are sometimes visited.

NORTHERN CARDINAL

Sheltered ground feeders and bin feeders on poles, both close to thick coniferous trees, hedgerows, or thickets are crucial to attracting northern cardinals into the backyard. The bright red birds have a definite sense of the vulnerability that comes with their plumage and respond by keeping close to cover.

Although they are a midsize songbird in the majority of backyard situations, northern cardinals actually are bullied by most other species, even those smaller than themselves. Separate feeders, with one closer to cover intended for the northern cardinals, often solves this problem. Oil-type sunflower seeds are the primary seed for northern cardinals, although some backyard birdwatchers have great success with safflower seeds and peanut hearts.

PINE WARBLER
Dendroica pinus
Family: Parulidae
Description: 5½"; olive-brown above, yellow throat and breast, white underside with streaks, two white bars on each wing.
Habitat: Coniferous forests, particularly pine.
Range: Breeds from southern Canada south to Gulf of Mexico, east of the Mississippi; winters from North Carolina south across Gulf of Mexico.
Nest: Plant fibers woven into small cup at tip of branch on pine tree, usually more than 20' off the ground.
Eggs: Greenish white spotted and blotched with brown, mostly at the larger end; 3 to 5 per clutch.
Song: Loose, lazy trill, similar to chipping sparrow but softer.
Other regions: SE and SC (extreme south).

NORTHERN CARDINAL
Cardinalis cardinalis
Family: Fringillidae
Description: 8 to 9"; male bright red with crest, black face; female dull yellow-brown tinted with red on crest, wings, and tail.
Habitat: Brushy areas and thickets.
Range: Southernmost Canada and the Dakotas south to Gulf of Mexico; also occurs in areas of the Southwest and southern California.
Nest: Twigs, leaves, and grass woven into cup in shrub or low tree in thick cover.
Eggs: Greenish or bluish white spotted and blotched with reddish brown; 3 to 4 per clutch.
Song: "Sweet-sweet-sweet-sweet."
Call: "Chip."
Other regions: SE, PP (eastern), SW (southern), PC (southern), and SC (southernmost).

45

AMERICAN TREE SPARROW

The number of tree sparrows at our feeders in any given winter is highly variable, determined by environmental factors. But unlike most finches of the North, the American tree sparrow's southern migration is dependent on weather rather than food supply. A mild winter in the North generally results in fewer birds south of the U.S.-Canadian border.

Nesting boxes erected in open field areas will be used by the birds, particularly if the fields are located near open water or wetlands. When one or more breeding pairs are attracted, the backyard bird-watcher will be treated to repeated aerial displays as courting males and females chase each other through the sky in series after series of gyrations.

TREE SPARROW

Tachycineta bicolor
Family: Fringillidae
Description: 5½ to 6½"; streaked brown above, gray below with dark gray spot at center of breast, gray head with red-brown crown.
Habitat: Agricultural areas, weedy edges at woodlands, thickets.
Range: Breeds in Alaska and northern Canada; winters in the northern half of the U.S.
Nest: Bits of bark and plant fibers woven into cup lined with hair, in low vegetation on the tundra.
Eggs: Light blue spotted with brown; 4 to 5 per clutch.
Song: Couple of clear notes and then a rapid warble.
Other regions: PP (northern), RM, and PC (extreme north).

WHITE-THROATED SPARROW

During the winter months almost every bit of thick cover seems to be packed with white-throated sparrows, one of our most common birds. Small flocks travel from feeder to feeder during the day, gathering into much larger flocks in the evening. They sometimes have the unusual habit of singing while in these winter flocks.

In spring, the white-throated sparrow shifts almost exclusively to the buds and blossoms of various trees, including maple,   , and beech, with the last mentioned a decided preference. Despite this habit, the species is not a major orchard pest.

PURPLE FINCH

Often confused with the more common house finch, the much redder purple finch is nonetheless a very numerous species. Large flocks of the small bird will frequent all feeders in a given neighborhood on a fairly regular schedule from day to day. The preferred seeds are oil-type sunflower and niger in hanging feeders.

Weeds seeds, particularly those of such especially noxious species as thistle and dandelion, comprise nearly all of the purple finch's diet. For this reason, corners and back edges of the backyard left untended to go to weedy growth are an excellent habitat approach to attracting this and most other finch species. Fruits make up a small, but relished, part of the bird's diet.

For other birds that might be sighted in backyards in the Northeast and Mid-Atlantic, refer to the following species in other chapters of this book:

Chapter One: Pancontinental Birds: All.

Chapter Three: Southeast: Eastern phoebe, eastern kingbird, eastern wood pewee, blue-gray gnatcatcher, gray catbird, black-and-white warbler, Kentucky warbler.

Chapter Four: Plains & Prairies: Bobolink, orchard oriole, indigo bunting, Henslow's sparrow, ovenbird, Louisiana waterthrush, prothonotary warbler.

Chapter Five: Southwest: Fox sparrow, hermit thrush.

Chapter Six: Rockies: Red crossbill, willow flycatcher, tree swallow, Swainson's thrush.

Chapter Seven: Pacific Coast: Winter wren, marsh wren, evening grosbeak, purple martin.

Chapter Eight: Southern Canada: American redstart, northern parula warbler, chestnut-sided warbler, rose-breasted grosbeak, wood thrush, scarlet tanager, rusty blackbird.

WHITE-THROATED SPARROW

Zonotrichia albicollis
Family: Fringillidae
Description: 6 to 7"; streaked in shades of gray-brown above, gray below, black and white stripes on head, patch of white on throat, yellow lores.
Habitat: Brushy areas within coniferous woodlands; also, in winter in agricultural and suburban areas.
Range: Breeds across Canada and in northeastern U.S.; winters from northeastern U.S. south across the Southeast and, in the West, along the southern Pacific Coast.
Nest: Grass, moss, and plant fibers woven into cup on or near ground in undergrowth.
Eggs: Bluish white spotted with brown; 4 to 5 per clutch.
Song: "Sweet-sweet-Canada-Canada."
Call: "Tseet."
Other regions: SE, PP (eastern), PC (southern), and SC.

PURPLE FINCH

Carpodacus purpureus
Family: Fringillidae
Description: 5½ to 6½"; male is dark red with faint brown streaks across back and sides; female is streaked in shades of brown, with noticeable light eyebrow.
Habitat: Woodlands of coniferous and mixed species, also residential areas with coniferous trees.
Range: Winters from southern Canada south to Gulf of Mexico, east of the Mississippi, and along the Pacific Coast in the West.
Nest: Grass and twigs woven into cup lined with hair, in a coniferous tree or shrub.
Eggs: Blue-green spotted and scrawled with brown and black at larger end; 3 to 5 per clutch.
Song: Clear warble ending in downward trill.
Call: "Tick" (while in flight).
Other regions: SE, PP (eastern), PC, and SC.

3.
Southeast

EASTERN WOOD PEWEE

Deciduous woodlands are the primary home of the eastern wood pewee, but backyards, parks, and the like that offer a substantial amount of heavy shade also are attractive. The bird spends a good deal of time perched on dead branches high atop the trees in wait for passing insects in flight.

In addition to insects, the eastern wood pewee eats some berries. It is not much of a feeder bird, but has been known to come to suet. Some backyard birdwatchers have reported success in attracting the species to birdbaths.

EASTERN PHOEBE

In the southeastern portion of the U.S., the eastern phoebe is mostly a year-round resident. In the northern states the species is a migrant, although it stays on later in the fall and returns earlier in the spring than most other songbirds.

Records indicate that the eastern phoebe was the first bird ever banded for scientific research. John James Audubon attached a small wire to one's leg in the fall of 1840 and duly recorded its return to Pennsylvania the next spring.

The covered areas under bridges are favored nesting areas and will be used by generation after generation of the birds. Backyards near such bridges are included in the birds' territory as they hunt for insects.

EASTERN WOOD PEWEE
Contopus virens
Family: nidae
Description: 6 to 7"; grayish olive, pair of white bars on each wing.
Habitat: Open wooded areas, from woodlands to parks.
Range: Breeds from southeastern Canada to Gulf of Mexico; winters in Central and South America.
Nest: Plant fibers woven into cup and camouflaged with lichen, attached across a tree limb.
Eggs: Milky white blotched with brown at larger end; 3 to 4 per clutch.
Song: "Pee-ah-wee."
Other regions: NE, PP (eastern), and SC (southern half).

EASTERN PHOEBE
Sayornis phoebe
Family: Tyrannidae
Description: 6½ to 7½"; dull olive green throughout.
Habitat: On cliffs, under bridges or eaves of houses, hollow trees, near streams.
Range: Breeds south as far as southern Canada, east of the Rockies; winters north as far as Virginia, eastern half of the U.S.
Nest: Grass cemented with mud and lined with hair, attached to ledges on buildings, bridges, cliffs, and the like or under the upturned roots of fallen trees.
Eggs: White; 3 to 6 per clutch.
Song: "Phee-be" (repeated).
Call: "Chip."
Other regions: NE, PP (eastern), and SC.

GREAT CRESTED FLYCATCHER
Myiarchus crinitus
Family: Tyrannidae
Description: 8½ to 9½"; brown above, gray throat, yellow underside, red-brown wings and tail, small crest.
Habitat: Open wooded areas and agricultural areas with large trees.
Range: Breeds from southern Canada south to Gulf of Mexico on the eastern half of the continent; winters from southern Mexico south to South America.
Nest: Twigs and plant fibers in loose arrangement lined with discarded items such as string, bits of cloth, plastic wrap, and snake skin, in a cavity.
Eggs: Milky white spotted and blotched with brown; 5 to 6 per clutch.
Song: "Wheep-wheep-wheep" (buzzingly).
Other regions: NE, PP (eastern), and SC (eastern).

GREAT CRESTED FLYCATCHER
Woodlands are the habitat of choice for the great crested flycatcher. Among the trees, the male establishes a large territory that it defends from all other males in aerial combat that often includes midair collision, clawing, and the ripping out of feathers. Any substantial stand of deciduous trees will serve this purpose.

Bird boxes are one of the most effective means to bring the great crested flycatcher, primarily an insect eater, into the backyard. The birds show a decided preference for cavities and nesting boxes with bottoms no more than eighteen inches lower than their entrance holes. They usually try to include bits of snake skin in the lining of their nest, but have adapted to the modern world and now put onion skins and cellophane to this use.

EASTERN KINGBIRD

The eastern kingbird is a highly aggressive species, quite willing to pummel much larger species like hawks and blue jays. This behavior, which will be especially severe near the kingbird's nest, helped to give the bird its regal name.

It is largely an insect eater, but also consumes large amounts of berries, taken from bushes while it flies. Early in the fall, kingbirds congregate into large flocks that fill the evening air in pursuit of insects.

EASTERN KINGBIRD

Tyrannus tyrannus
Family: Tyrannidae
Description: 8 to 9"; dark gray above, darker at head, white below, black tail with white tip, red patch on crown (not usually displayed).
Habitat: Open areas, ranging from farmlands to lake shores.
Range: Breeds from central Canada south to the southern U.S. in the East and central U.S. in the West; winters in South America.
Nest: Loose mass of twigs lined with plant fibers and hair, in low tree or shrub.
Eggs: Milky white blotched with brown and black; 3 to 5 per clutch.
Song: "Dtzee-dtzee-dtzeet" (very sharply).
Other regions: NE, PP (northern half), RM, and SC.

CAROLINA CHICKADEE

Parus carolinensis

Family: Paridae

Description: 4 to 5"; gray above, white below, black cap and throat, white cheeks.

Habitat: Deciduous woodlands and residential areas with deciduous trees.

Range: Central U.S. south to Gulf of Mexico.

Nest: Grass, plant fibers, and feathers jammed into cavity.

Eggs: White spotted with red-brown, mostly at larger end; 6 to 8 per clutch.

Song: "Fee-bee-bee-bay."

Call: "Chickadee-dee-dee-dee."

54

CAROLINA CHICKADEE

The Carolina chickadee occurs in part of the same range as the very similar-looking black-capped chickadee, for which it is often confused. But the two species are highly competitive in the breeding season and generally do not overlap on the same territories within their ranges.

The Carolina chickadee shares its cousin's habit as a common and regular feeder visitor. Where it supplants the black-capped chickadee, it is a member of the mixed flocks of chickadees, titmice, nuthatches, small woodpeckers, and kinglets.

BLUE-GRAY GNATCATCHER

The blue-gray gnatcatcher appears to be constantly in motion, as it searches the treetops for insects or dives to take them on the wing. It consumes a wide variety of insect and spider species, including their eggs and larvae.

Such activity is readily interrupted the moment the blue-gray gnatcatcher hears either a squeaking noise or an owl call, which it immediately sets out to investigate. This inquisitive bird approaches quite closely in its search for the exact source of the noise.

BLUE-GRAY GNATCATCHER
Polioptila caerulea
Family: Sylviidae
Description: 4½ to 5"; blue-gray above, white below and around eyes, black tail with white edges, long tail.
Habitat: Open and damp wooded areas, especially along streams with heavy undergrowth.
Range: Breeds from southernmost Canada south to Gulf of Mexico and into Central America; winters north as far as the southern two-thirds of the U.S.
Nest: Very small plant fibers, plant down, spider web wove into cup attached to tree limb.
Eggs: Light blue spotted with red-brown; 4 to 5 per clutch.
Song: "Pzzzz" (nasally).
Other regions: NE, PP (eastern), SW, PC, and SC (southernmost).

GRAY CATBIRD

Mostly an insect eater, the gray catbird is most readily attracted into backyards with an array of dense thickets and hedgerows. From these secluded locations, its catlike meowing and its mimicking of the songs of other birds will fill the air.

The bird also eats its fill of grapes and berries, when they are available. At the feeder, preferably close to thick vegetation, the birds accept raisins, currants, cereals, bread crumbs, and bits of cheese.

GRAY CATBIRD
Dumetella carolinensis
Family: Mimidae
Description: 8 to 9¼"; dark gray throughout except for black cap and red-brown undertail feathers, long tail.
Habitat: Brushy areas.
Range: Breeds from southern Canada south to Gulf of Mexico; winters from central U.S. south through Central America.
Nest: Twigs, leaves, and plant stems in loose mass lined with softer plant fibers in thick brush or vines.
Eggs: Greenish blue; 3 to 5 per clutch.
Song: Long series of mechanical notes, each phrase only once; also mimics other bird calls.
Call: "Meeow."
Other regions: NE, PP, RM, and SC.

BROWN THRASHER
Toxostoma rufum
Family: Mimidae
Description: 10½ to 12"; red-brown above, white below streaked with brown, curved bill, long tail.
Habitat: Brushy areas, including old fields overgrown with shrubs and woodland edges.
Range: Breeds from southern Canada (eastern half) south to Gulf of Mexico; winters in the southeastern quarter of the U.S.
Nest: Twigs, leaves, and plant fibers in loosely woven bowl lined with grass, close to ground in thick shrub.
Eggs: Pale bluish white daintily spotted with red-brown; 3 to 5 per clutch.
Song: Various musical notes, each repeated twice.
Call: "Smack," followed by 3 whistled notes.
Other regions: NE, SE, and SC.

BROWN THRASHER

Although the brown thrasher's brown-and-white plumage won't win it any beauty contests, the bird's habit of tossing leaf litter hither and yon with its bill while searching for insects has endeared it to many backyard birdwatchers. A hedgerow or thicket with a thick layer of leaves underneath is especially attractive to this relatively shy species—all the more so if that spot is along the edge of a wooded area.

The brown thrasher is not as accomplished at mimicry as the northern mockingbird or catbird, but it does imitate the calls of several species, much to the agitation of these birds.

BLACK-AND-WHITE WARBLER

Mniotilta varia
Family: Parulidae
Description: 4½ to 5½"; striped in black and white; male has black throat, female has white throat.
Habitat: Deciduous woodlands; also, in migration, residential areas with trees and shrubs.
Range: Breeds from southern Canada south to the southern U.S., except for the Deep South, east of the Rockies; winters from Gulf of Mexico south to South America.
Nest: Grass, plant fibers, and leaves loosely woven and lined with hair and plant down, on ground at base of tree, rock, or similar backing.
Eggs: White spotted with brown; 4 to 5 per clutch.
Song: "Weesy-weesy-weesy-weesy" (high pitched).
Other regions: NE, PP, and SC.

BLACK-AND-WHITE WARBLER

Once known as the black-and-white creeper for its habit of creeping about on the sides of tree trunks, the black-and-white warbler incorporates the practices of both the brown creeper and the nuthatches to hop both up and headfirst down the tree. (See these other species in Chapter Two, "Northeast & Mid-Atlantic.")

With habits that are much closer to those of the creepers and nuthatches than to other warblers, the black-and-white warbler often travels with the mixed winter flocks of those other species. This often brings the species into closer proximity to human beings than many other warbler species.

KENTUCKY WARBLER

The name of the Kentucky warbler would seem to indicate that the state is overrun with the bird. However, there is no evidence to suggest that Kentucky has any more or less of the bird than other states within the species' range. Instead, the name actually refers to the place where Alexander Wilson discovered the species in 1811.

Thickets and dense hedgerows are essential to attracting the Kentucky warbler, which prefers to live as secretively as it can. Such thick vegetation along waterways is particularly attractive.

KENTUCKY WARBLER

Oporornis formosus
Family: Parulidae
Description: 5 to 6"; olive green above, yellow below and around eyes; black on crown, between eyes, and at sides of throat.
Habitat: Damp woodland with heavy undergrowth.
Range: Breeds across the southern two-thirds of the eastern U.S.; winters from southern Mexico south to South America.
Nest: Loose gathering of dead leaves lined with grass and hair, on or very close to ground.
Eggs: White spotted and blotched with brown and gray, mostly at larger end; 4 to 5 per clutch.
Song: "Tur-eee, tur-eee, tur-eee, tur-eee" (loudly).
Other regions: NE (southern) and PP (eastern).

EASTERN MEADOWLARK

Sturnella magna
Family: Icteridae
Description: 9 to 11";
streaked in shades of brown
with bright yellow throat and
breast (crossed by black "V")
and white edges at tail.
Habitat: Grassy, weedy
areas.
Range: Breeds from southeastern Canada south to Gulf
of Mexico and in southwestern
U.S.; winters as far north at
New England and Nebraska.
Nest: Partially domed basket
of grass, in depression in a
meadow.
Eggs: White spotted with
brown and lavender, mostly at
larger end; 3 to 7 per clutch.
Song: "See-you, see-yeeer."
Other regions: NE, PP (eastern), SW (southeastern), and
SC (southeastern).

PAINTED BUNTING

Passerina ciris
Family: Fringillidae
Description: 5 to 6"; male is
brilliant red on its underside
and rump, green on its back,
and purple on its head with a
red eye ring; female is green
throughout, but paler below.
Habitat: Brushy areas,
hedgerows, thickets, woodland
edges.
Range: Southeastern U.S.
west to Texas.
Nest: Grass, plant fibers, and
strips of bark woven into cup
lined with plant fibers and
hair, in small tree or shrub.
Eggs: White spotted with red-
brown; 3 to 5 per clutch.
Song: High-pitched, tinkling.
Call: "Tsick."
Other regions: PP (eastern).

EASTERN MEADOWLARK

A classic subject of American farming lore and legend, the eastern meadowlark is a bird of hay fields and meadows. As such, the backyard that borders on these agricultural areas is most likely to include the bird in its population.

Those lucky residents whose backyards fulfill this requirement can encourage a close proximity to the cheerful whistle of the eastern meadowlark by offering a conspicuous perch, where the male prefers to sing during the spring.

Where one female is discovered to be nesting, chances are good that a second and even more can also be found. The male is polygamous and often attracts several females into his territory for breeding.

PAINTED BUNTING

Dense thickets or hedgerows are essential for any backyard birdwatcher hoping to attract the painted bunting. This brilliantly colored little bird sticks to the thickest cover it can find.

Despite the eye-catching red, green, and purple coloration of the males of this species, the birdwatcher's best hopes for spotting the bird is during the spring, when it mounts an exposed perch upon which to sing. The male is a persistent singer and will remain on its perch for lengthy sessions. It is readily attracted to seed feeders.

For other birds that might be sighted in backyards in the Southeast, refer to the following species in other chapters of the book:
   Chapter One: Pancontinental Birds: All.
   Chapter Two: Northeast & Mid-Atlantic: Blue jay, northern cardinal, white-throated sparrow, purple finch, eastern bluebird, brown creeper, white-breasted nuthatch, tufted titmouse.
   Chapter Four: Plains & Prairies: Bobolink, orchard oriole, indigo bunting, Henslow's sparrow, ovenbird, Louisiana waterthrush, vermilion flycatcher.
   Chapter Five: Southwest: Fox sparrow, summer tanager, hermit thrush.
   Chapter Six: Rockies: Red crossbill, tree swallow.
   Chapter Seven: Pacific Coast: Winter wren, marsh wren, water pipit, purple martin.
   Chapter Eight: Southern Canada: American redstart, northern parula warbler, chestnut-sided warbler, black-throated blue warbler, rose-breasted grosbeak, wood thrush, rusty blackbird.

4.
Plains & Prairies

VERMILION FLYCATCHER

Relatively tame for a flycatcher, the vermilion flycatcher is quite at home building its nest and raising its young near buildings. It prefers locales that offer readily and constantly available water sources, such as streams, animal troughs, and birdbaths. Thicket areas are another desirable habitat element.

The male of the species engages in a captivating courtship flight song, springing from a low perch to climb dozens of feet into the air. There it hovers, resembling a miniature hawk, drifting in small circles and periodically twittering. Finally, it circles down to its intended mate in dense weeds and the two fly together to the nesting site.

RED-EYED VIREO

Sometimes occurring in densities of as much as one breeding pair per acre, the red-eyed vireo is one of the most abundant birds east of the Mississippi.

It is also one of the noisiest. From dawn to dusk, even on days when other species opt for silence, the male red-eyed vireo will pour forth its robinlike song. The song's ventriloquial quality, coupled with the bird's habit of moving so little, makes it difficult to locate even the most persistent singer.

VERMILION FLYCATCHER
Pyrocephalus rubinus
Family: Tyrannidae
Description: 5½ to 6½"; male is bright red with dark brown on back, wings, and tail; female is white with dark brown streaks where male is bright red.
Habitat: Open areas with scattered trees and shrubs.
Range: Breeds across the southern third of the U.S., east as far as Florida and west as far as California; winters from the southern edge of the U.S. south to South America.
Nest: Plant fibers, spider silk, and feathers woven into cup lined with bits of lichen, on tree branch.
Eggs: Milky white spotted with dark brown; 3 per clutch.
Song: "T-t-t-t-zee."
Call: "Peet-peet."
Other regions: SE and SW (southern).

RED-EYED VIREO
Vireo olivaceus
Family: Vireonidae
Description: 5½ to 6½"; brown-green above, off-white below, white eyebrows, gray crown, red eyes.
Habitat: Woodlands of deciduous trees; residential areas with deciduous trees.
Range: Breeds from central Canada south to Gulf of Mexico, from the Rockies east; winters in South America.
Nest: Plant fibers and bits of bark woven into cup, covered with lichen bits and attached to twig of tree.
Eggs: White spotted with brown and black; 2 to 4 per clutch.
Song: "Here-I-am, where-are-you, here-I-am, where-are-you."
Other regions: NE, SE, RM (northern), and SC.

PROTHONOTARY WARBLER

The name of this golden bird of the wetlands is a corruption of the word *Protonotarius*, the traditional designation of yellow-robed officials in the Vatican.

Along with the Lucy's warbler, the prothonotary warbler has the distinction of being one of the two species of the Parulidae family that locates its nest in cavities. It is a very active bird, and nearly every nook and cranny of its chosen territory receives at least one visit per day.

OVENBIRD

Little can be done to bring the ovenbird into the backyard, short of locating the property adjacent to the woodlands that the small bird calls home. Although rarely seen in backyards that do not meet this criteria, the ovenbird is a very common species within its habitat.

The bird takes its name from the Dutch ovenlike, domed nest that it hides among the vegetation and leaf litter on the forest floor. The nest is among the most difficult of any bird's to locate, even when the nesting bird is observed performing its "injured bird" routine to deter the intruder.

LOUISIANA WATERTHRUSH

As its name implies, the Louisiana waterthrush prefers a habitat that includes a body of water, particularly fast-moving streams. A part of the bird's routine is to wade into the more shallow areas in search of insects and small invertebrates hidden under the leaf litter.

The Louisiana waterthrush is generally an early spring arrival as well as one of the first species to leave for its southward flight in the fall. It usually departs its summers haunts by late August.

OVENBIRD
Seiurus aurocapillus
Family: Parulidae
Description: 5½ to 6½"; brownish green above, white below streaked with brown, burnt orange crown edged with black stripes, pink legs.
Habitat: Open, mature woodlands.
Range: Breeds from central Canada south across the northern two-thirds of the U.S., in the eastern half of the continent; winters from Gulf of Mexico to South America.
Nest: Plant fibers and dead leaves woven into domed basket with side entrance, on ground.
Eggs: White spotted with red-brown; 3 to 6 per clutch.
Song: "Teacher, teacher, teacher" (loudly).
Other regions: NE, SE (northern), and SC (eastern).

PROTHONOTARY WARBLER
Protonotaria citrea
Family: Parulidae
Description: 5 to 5½"; male is yellow on the head, neck, breast, and underside, greenish olive on the back, and bluish gray on the wings; female is a duller version.
Habitat: Damp woodlands, swamps, and stream sides.
Range: Northeastern U.S. west into the Great Plains.
Nest: Grass, moss, leaves, and twigs woven into cup lined with fine plant fibers and feathers, in tree cavity.
Eggs: Cream-colored spotted with brown and gray; 3 to 8 per clutch.
Song: "Peet, sweet, sweet, sweet, sweet, sweet."
Other regions: NE.

LOUISIANA WATERTHRUSH
Seiurus motacilla
Family: Parulidae
Description: 6 to 7"; dark green-brown above, white streaked with green-brown below, no streaking on throat, white eyebrows.
Habitat: Along bodies of water and swampy areas.
Range: Breeds from southern Canada south to Georgia and Texas; winters from Mexico south to South America.
Nest: Moss and dead leaves in loose mass lined with grass under stream bank overhang or in cavity of tree stump.
Eggs: White spotted and blotched with brown; 4 to 6 per clutch.
Song: Three clear notes and then a descending mishmash.
Other regions: NE (southern) and SE (not Deep South).

INDIGO BUNTING

Passerina cyanea

Family: Fringillidae

Description: 5 to 6"; in direct sunlight, male is shimmering turquoise blue; under other light conditions, male is dark blue with darker wings and tail; female is dark brown, lighter below.

Habitat: Brushy, overgrown areas; also woodland edges next to fields.

Range: Breeds from southern Canada south to Gulf of Mexico, across the eastern half of the continent, and in scattered areas of the southwestern U.S.; winters from Mexico south through Central America.

Nest: Grass and leaves woven into cup, in small tree or shrub in dense cover.

Eggs: Bluish white; 2 to 6 per clutch.

Song: "Tee-tee-tyu-tyu-shoe-shoe-tee-tee-wee-wee."

Other regions: NE, SE, SE (scattered areas), and SC.

INDIGO BUNTING

Although there is no blue pigment in the plumage of the indigo bunting, when the sun hits the male just right it literally glows with brilliant turquoise blue. The bird's coloring is actually black, but diffraction of sunlight by the feathers gives it this special coloration.

The indigo bunting has benefited from the failure of small family farms and the subsequent recovery of the land by thick brush and second-growth woodlands. This trend has worked to increase the range of the species to the west and south.

DICKCISSEL

Most of the U.S. population of dickcissels spends the winter months south of the U.S.-Mexican border, but a substantial number also winter in the U.S. Here they become regular feeder visitors, joining inconspicuously into flocks of house sparrows. Oil-type sunflower seeds, cracked corn, and grains are the preferred feeder foods.

DICKCISSEL

Spiza americana
Family: Fringillidae
Description: 5½ to 6½"; male has a brown back streaked with black, yellow breast crossed by a black "V" and red-brown patches on its wings; female has yellow throat and breast and faint streaking along her sides.
Habitat: Open or weedy agricultural areas.
Range: Breeds from the Canadian to the Mexican border across the middle of the U.S.; winters from Mexico south to South America.
Nest: Plant fibers and grass woven into cup on or close to the ground, in agricultural field.
Eggs: Light blue; 3 to 5 per clutch.
Song: "Dick-dick-ssissel" (continuously repeated).

LARK BUNTING

When one pair of lark buntings finds suitable habitat for nesting—open fields and grasslands—additional pairs generally can be expected to follow. The species is much more accepting of nesting in close proximity with others of its kind than most birds. Just a couple of acres of suitable habitat often will hold several breeding pairs. In these locations, the birdwatcher can spot several males on any given evening, launching themselves into the air to perform their courtship flight songs. This habit seems to have evolved because of the lack of suitable singing perches across much of the bird's range.

Winter months will see the species mass into flocks of hundreds that can be attracted to any large offering of grain.

HENSLOW'S SPARROW

A few patches of weeds scattered along the edges of a backyard lawn offers perfect habitat for the Henslow's sparrow. The several pairs that such landscape features attract will stick pretty close to the sanctuary of the weed patches, through which they will run—rather than fly—when threatened.

However, perfect habitat is no guarantee of attracting the birds. For reasons that are as yet unexplained the birds are present in colonies of as many as a dozen pairs in one locality but absent from another locality that appears to offer exactly the same habitat.

The backyard birdwatcher's best opportunity for sighting these small birds is when they perch on a weed stalk to sing.

LARK BUNTING
Calamospiza melanocorys
Family: Fringillidae
Description: 6 to 7½"; male is black with white patches on wings; female is duller black streaked with brown.
Habitat: Open, grassy and weedy areas.
Range: Breeds from southern Canada (inner continent) south to Texas; winters from southern Texas south to central Mexico.
Nest: Twigs and grass woven into loose cup lined with hair, on ground in thick patch of weeds.
Eggs: Light blue; 2 to 6 per clutch.
Song: Series of varied trills.
Other regions: SW (southern).

HENSLOW'S SPARROW
Ammodramus henslowii
Family: Fringillidae
Description: 4½ to 5½"; brownish-streaked breast, olive green head, red-brown back.
Habitat: Grassy areas with scattered shrubs and weed patches.
Range: Breeds across the eastern half of the U.S.; winters in the southern Atlantic states and along Gulf of Mexico.
Nest: Grass woven into cup on ground, in tuft of grass.
Eggs: Off-white spotted with reddish brown; 3 to 5 per clutch.
Song: "Tsi-lick" (like a sneeze).
Other regions: NE and SE.

BOBOLINK

Dolichonyx oryzivorus
Family: Icteridae
Description: 6 to 8"; breeding male is black throughout with a white rump and underside and pale yellow at back of neck; female and male in winter are streaked with brownish yellow across back and crown.
Habitat: Grassy, weedy areas.
Range: Breeds from southern Canada south through the northern U.S.; winters in South America.
Nest: Grass and plant fibers woven very loosely into cup on ground, hidden in thick grass or weeds.
Eggs: Cream-colored to brown spotted and blotched with red-brown; 4 to 7 per clutch.
Song: Series of notes, each on different pitch and faster than preceding one.
Call: "Plink-plink" (often in flight).
Other regions: NE, SE, RM (northern), and SC.

BOBOLINK

The decline in small family farms across most of the U.S. has brought about a corresponding decline in our bobolink population. The bird with the name that's so much fun to say initially expanded as Europeans settled and cleared away the forest for fields. But now many farms have been abandoned, and as they return to woodlands the bobolink's preferred habitat is disappearing.

ORCHARD ORIOLE

Throughout much of its range, the orchard oriole is a familiar inhabitant of backyards and parks that offer a variety of shade tree species. Substantial colonies of more than a hundred breeding pairs are not uncommon in these areas, which the birds proceed to fill with their song from early spring to early summer.

Like its close relative the northern oriole, this species will readily accept short strands of yarn or string set out in hanging baskets. Birdbaths are a definite advantage for the backyard birdwatcher attempting to attract the orchard oriole.

ORCHARD ORIOLE

Icterus spurius

Family: Icteridae

Description: 6½ to 7½"; male is red-brown with black on head, back, wings and tail; female is yellowish green.

Habitat: Open areas with scattered trees and shrubs, especially near bodies of water.

Range: Breeds from northern U.S. south throughout the country and into northern Mexico; winters from Mexico south to South America.

Nest: Grass and plant fibers woven into a flexible basket hanging from tree branch.

Eggs: Pale bluish white blotched and scrawled with brown and purple; 4 to 6 per clutch.

Song: Rapid warble, ending in a downward "whew" note.

Other regions: NE and SE.

For other birds that might be sighted in backyards in the Plains & Prairies region, refer to the following species in other chapters of this book:

Chapter One: Pancontinental Birds: All.

Chapter Two: Northeast & Mid-Atlantic: Blue jay, northern cardinal, white-throated sparrow, American tree sparrow, purple finch, eastern bluebird, brown creeper, red-breasted nuthatch, white-breasted nuthatch, black-capped chickadee, tufted titmouse.

Chapter Three: Southeast: Eastern phoebe, eastern kingbird, eastern wood pewee, painted bunting, great crested flycatcher, blue-gray gnatcatcher, gray catbird, black-and-white warbler, Kentucky warbler, eastern meadowlark.

Chapter Five: Southwest: Say's phoebe, fox sparrow, summer tanager, Bell's vireo.

Chapter Six: Rockies: Lazuli bunting, red crossbill, black-headed grosbeak, willow flycatcher, tree swallow, western tanager.

Chapter Seven: Pacific Coast: Winter wren, evening grosbeak, yellow-headed blackbird, water pipit, purple martin.

Chapter Eight: Southern Canada: Northern parula warbler, rose-breasted grosbeak, wood thrush, scarlet tanager, rusty blackbird.

5. Southwest

SAY'S PHOEBE

A sheltered nesting ledge in many areas of the Southwest will often attract the mud-ball-and-grass nest of the Say's phoebe. The man-made structure is taken by the bird as a substitute for the cliffs and canyon walls along which it otherwise nests.

Although the species is very migratory to southern climes in the winter, some individuals remain behind through the colder months. Berries offered at the feeder very often will attract these birds.

PLAIN TITMOUSE

Two separate species of the plain titmouse occupy the opposite sides of the Sierra Nevada Mountains, with the only major difference being in slight color variation and habitat choices. Both races are attracted to oil-type sunflower seeds and peanut butter at the feeder. In addition, both races will quickly set up housekeeping in natural snags, holes in fence posts, and small bird boxes.

SAY'S PHOEBE
Sayornis saya
Family: Tyrannidae
Description: 7 to 9"; gray-brown on back, black tail and red-brown underside.
Habitat: Open country, plains, cliffs, badlands.
Range: Breeds from Alaska and central Canada south to Texas and Mexico; winters in southern California and the southwestern U.S.
Nest: Grasses, mosses, plant stems, spider silk arranged in flat structure, in cavities or on ledges.
Eggs: White; 3 to 7 per clutch.
Song: "Pippety-chee."
Call: "Phee-eur."
Other regions: PP, PC, and SC (western).

PLAIN TITMOUSE
Parus inornatus
Family: Paridae
Description: 5 to 6"; gray-brown above, pale gray to off-white below, conspicuous crest.
Habitat: Open areas or foothills with oak, pinyon, or juniper trees.
Range: Rockies west to the Pacific Coast.
Nest: Leaves, bark strips, mosses, hair, and snake skin stuffed into cavity.
Eggs: White spotted with shades of brown; 5 to 8 per clutch.
Song: "Peter-peter-peter."
Call: "Day-day-day."
Other regions: RM, PC, and SC (western).

CACTUS WREN

Campylorchynchus brunneicapillus
Family: Troglodytidae
Description: 8 to 8¼"; brown, spotted below, white over eyes and in spots on tail, red-brown crown.
Habitat: Cacti areas and thickets in the desert.
Range: Southern California east to Texas and south to Central America.
Nest: Grass and plant fibers woven into ball with side entrance, lined with hair and feathers, on top of cactus or thorn-laden shrub.
Eggs: Pinkish yellow spotted with brown; 4 to 5 per clutch.
Song: "Chug-chug-chug-chug-chug" (mechanically).
Other regions: PP (extreme southwest).

CACTUS WREN

As its name reveals, the cactus wren generally is found only where cacti occur in good numbers. The nests of the birds, including several "dummy" nests that are used only as roosts as well as the actual breeding nest, are scattered about the cacti where the species lives. It sometimes nests among extremely thorny shrubs in lieu of cacti.

The cactus wren, the state bird of Arizona, is a common resident around buildings, where it is quite at home hunting for its insect prey on the lawns.

CANYON WREN

Like most wren species, the canyon wren enjoys its privacy and secrecy. Hearing the bird's tittering song is just the beginning of what generally must be a time-consuming and careful search.

The bird prefers rocky areas, such as cliffs and canyons, as a major portion of its environment. It is an adept rock climber, with a body well adapted to squeezing into crevices, although old stone structures and rock piles often attract its attention as well. Pairs have even been known to build their nests in occupied homes.

AMERICAN DIPPER

Clean freshwater streams are the critical factor in habitat choice of the American dipper. Much of the bird's food comes from such aquatic sources, located as the American dipper struts from rock to rock along the water's edge. When it finds a likely spot, the American dipper wades directly into the water, submerges its body, and walks along the bottom, using its wings to fight the current. With a morsel secured, the bird erupts from the water and flies to a perch.

Winter finds the American dipper wherever the water remains open, often at lower elevations on the same stream it inhabited in the mountains during the warmer months.

CANYON WREN
Catherpes mexicanus
Family: Troglodytidae
Description: 5½ to 6"; dark red-brown with white throat and breast.
Habitat: Canyons with plenty of exposed rocks, cliffs, stone buildings.
Range: Western half of the U.S., except for the Northwest.
Nest: Plant fibers, moss, and feathers woven into cup, in a crevice between rocks.
Eggs: White spotted with red-brown; 4 to 6 per clutch.
Song: "Tee-tee-tee-tee-tew-tew-tew-tew."
Other regions: PC (southern) and RM.

AMERICAN DIPPER
Cinclus mexicanus
Family: Cinclidae
Description: 7 to 8½"; dark gray throughout with white on upper eyelids and black bill, indistinct spots on breast.
Habitat: Along swift, freshwater streams.
Range: Western North America.
Nest: Mosses and grasses fashioned into ovenlike shape always near stream, sometimes beneath waterfall or on rock in midstream.
Eggs: White; 3 to 6 per clutch.
Song: Bubbling, wrenlike notes.
Other regions: SW, RM, PC, and SC (western).

RUBY-CROWNED KINGLET

RUBY-CROWNED KINGLET

Regulus calendula
Family: Sylviidae
Description: 3¾ to 4½"; olive green throughout with pair of white bars on each wing and white rings around the eyes; male also has red on crown that usually is not exposed.
Habitat: Woodlands of coniferous trees; in winter, also in other types of woodlands.
Range: Breeds from Alaska and central Canada south through Canada and the U.S. West; winters along the Pacific Coast and in the southern third of the U.S., north to New England in the East.
Nest: Plant fibers, moss, and lichen in large bundle with feather-lined cup at the top.
Eggs: Cream-colored spotted with red-brown, mostly at larger end; 6 to 9 per clutch.
Song: Chattering (loudly).

HERMIT THRUSH

Catharus guttatus
Family: Turdidae
Description: 6½ to 7½"; brown throughout with spotting on underside.
Habitat: Woodlands with thickets.
Range: Breeds from Alaska and central Canada south as far as Virginia in the mountains of the East, along the Rockies and the northern Pacific Coast; winter from the southern third of the U.S. south through Central America.
Nest: Leaves, plant fibers and moss woven into cup on or near ground, in woodlands.
Eggs: Pale blue-green; 3 to 4 per clutch.
Song: Series of musical phrases, each of different pitch.
Call: "Chuck."
Other regions: NE, SE, PP (southern), PC (northern), RM, and SC.

RUBY-CROWNED KINGLET

Insects and spiders form the bulk of the ruby-crowned kinglet's diet. But in the leaner months of winter, the bird supplements this fare with a variety of berries and seeds. It becomes a regular feeder visitor at this time.

Throughout much of the U.S., the ruby-crowned kinglet is primarily a migratory visitor each spring and fall, moving through in flocks of a few dozen—often with various warbler species. During these flights, the birds are likely to be found in nearly any setting or habitat.

HERMIT THRUSH

Many bird enthusiasts consider the reedy song of the hermit thrush to be the most beautiful of any North American songbird. Generally, however, the backyard setting is not treated to that wonderful melody. Woodlands, particularly of coniferous species, are the bird's normal haunts. Only rarely has the insect-eating hermit thrush been attracted to feeders.

A feeding hermit thrush bounces across the ground in the same manner as the robin, its cousin. It frequently stops and stands motionless for a few seconds, turning over leaf after leaf in search of insects or strays bits of food, such as berries. The bird always uses its head and neck—never its feet—in the process.

BELL'S VIREO
Vireo belii
Family: Vireonidae
Description: 4¾ to 5"; greenish brown above, off-white below, white eye rings and wing bars.
Habitat: Thick bottomland and mesquite areas.
Range: Breeds throughout the U.S. Southwest and central U.S.; winters in Central and South America.
Nest: Plant fibers and bits of bark woven into cup, in thickly leaved shrub or tree.
Eggs: White spotted with brown; 3 to 5 per clutch.
Song: "Tweedle-deedle-dum" (questioningly, immediately followed by) "tweedle-deedle-dee" (with excitement).
Other regions: PP.

PYRRHULOXIA
Cardinalis sinuatus
Family: Fringillidae
Description: 7½ to 8½"; male light gray with red breast, wings and tail; female lacks red on breast; parrotlike yellow bill.
Habitat: Brushy areas of desert, especially near waterways.
Range: Southern California east to southern Texas and south to central Mexico.
Nest: Grass, bits of bark and twigs woven into loose cup, in thick shrub.
Eggs: White spotted with brown; 3 to 4 per clutch.
Song: "Purty-purty-purty."
Call: "Chip."
Other regions: PC (extreme south).

BELL'S VIREO

The nests of the Bell's vireo are one of the primary western victims of the cowbird's practice of laying its eggs in the nests of other birds and abandoning them there for care by the unknowing foster parents. However, this practice is not very successful when it comes to the Bell's vireo, as the bird simply abandons the nest when the cowbird egg appears.

Audubon named this species for John Bell, who accompanied him during his 1840 travels along the Missouri River.

PYRRHULOXIA

Mesquite is extremely attractive to the pyrrhuloxia, the strangely named cousin of the northern cardinal. The bird relishes the tender insides of the mesquite bean, which it cracks open in its strong bill.

While the overall range of the pyrrhuloxia is quite limited, where it occurs it generally is very common across many different habitat types. Except for the breeding season, the bird travels in small groups, actively seeking out sources of seeds. Feeders, particularly those offering oil-type sunflower seeds and cracked corn, are readily accepted.

SUMMER TANAGER

The summer tanager is by no means a true feeder bird. But those individual birds that miss the call of migration in the fall will eagerly become cold-weather regulars at any feeder that offers fruit (particularly citrus), suet, and sunflower seeds, in that order.

SUMMER TANAGER

Piranga rubra
Family: Thraupidae
Description: 7 to 8"; male is red with black wings and tail, and a yellow bill; female is light olive green above and brownish yellow below.
Habitat: Woodlands with limited undergrowth and residential areas with ample deciduous trees.
Range: Breeds in the U.S. Southeast and Southwest; winters from southern Mexico south to South America.
Nest: Plant fibers woven very loosely into cup near end of tree limb, 10 to 20' off the ground.
Eggs: Blue-green spotted and blotched with brown; 3 to 4 per clutch.
Song: "Cheerily, cheer-up, cheerily."
Call: "Chick-burr."
Other regions: SE and PP (extreme southeast).

GREEN-TAILED TOWHEE

The green-tailed towhee is a strongly migratory species, although individuals readily stray far from their normal routes of migration. Because of this habit there is virtually no area of the U.S. that can be completely ruled out as a potential sighting location for a few of these birds. It eats a wide variety of seeds, and wanderers often find their way to backyard feeders.

FOX SPARROW

Western members of the fox sparrow species are much grayer than their reddish-brown eastern counterparts. However, they share the habit of scratching for insects in leaf litter so intensely and loudly as to give the impression of a much larger creature moving through the leaves. They also are attracted to the oil-type sunflower seeds offered on a platform or ground feeder.

GREEN-TAILED TOWHEE
Pipilo chlorurus
Family: Fringillidae
Description: 6 to 7"; greenish oliv on back, wings, and tail; red-brown crown, white throat, gray breast an face, yellow edges on wings.
Habitat: Weedy, shrubby areas.
Range: Breeds throughout western U.S.; winters from southwesternmost U.S. south into northern Mexico.
Nest: Grass, bits of bark and plant stems woven into cup lined with hair and softer plant fibers, at base of ca tus or thorny shrub.
Eggs: White spotted with brown; 2 5 per clutch.
Song: "Wheat-chur-cheeee-chur."
Call: "Chink."
Other regions: RM, PC, and SC (western).

FOX SPARROW
Passerella iliaca
Family: Fringillidae
Description: 6½ to 7½";
streaked in shades of red-brown
and off-white above, white spotted with red-brown below, red-
brown stripes on sides of gray
head, red-brown tail.
Habitat: Woodland undergrowth, particularly coniferous
areas; also, weedy grasslands.
Range: Breeds from Alaska
south to Mexico in the West and
south as far as central Canada in
the East; winters along the Pacific
Coast and the Southwest in the
West and throughout the eastern
half of the U.S.
Nest: Leaves, grass, and moss
woven into heavy-walled cup on
or close to the ground, in thick
brush.
Eggs: Light green spotted with
red-brown; 4 to 5 per clutch.
Song: Short warble.
Other regions: NE, SE, PP
(eastern), RM, PC, and SC
(western).

*For other birds that might be
sighted in backyards in the
Southwest, refer to the following
species in other chapters of the
book:*
Chapter One:
Pancontinental Birds: All.
Chapter Two: Northeast &
Mid-Atlantic: Blue jay,
northern cardinal, white-
breasted nuthatch.
Chapter Three: Southeast:
Blue-gray gnatcatcher, eastern
meadowlark.
Chapter Four: Plains &
Prairies: Lark bunting,
vermilion flycatcher.
Chapter Six: Rockies:
Black-headed grosbeak,
western tanager.
Chapter Seven: Pacific
Coast: Winter wren, marsh
wren, mountain bluebird,
evening grosbeak, yellow-
headed blackbird, water pipit,
purple martin.

6.
Rockies

OLIVE-SIDED FLYCATCHER
Contopus borealis
Family: Tyrannidae
Description: 7 to 8"; green-brown, darker at sides of breast and on flanks, white through center of breast, white tufts at base of tail, large head.
Habitat: Coniferous forests, generally near openings.
Range: Breeds from Alaska and central Canada south through the Rockies and Appalachians and along the Pacific Coast; winters in South America.
Nest: Loose collection of twigs lined with grass, moss, and lichen, in coniferous tree.
Eggs: Creamy white spotted and blotched with brown; 3 per clutch.
Song: "Quick-three-beers."
Call: "Pip-pip-pip."

TREE SWALLOW
Iridoprocne bicolor
Family: Hirundinidae
Description: 5 to 6¼"; silvery blue or shimmering blue-green above, white below.
Habitat: Along bodies of water.
Range: Breeds from Alaska and central Canada south along the U.S. coasts and mountain ranges; winters from the Carolinas and southern California south to Gulf of Mexico and Mexico.
Nest: Grass woven into cup lined with feathers, in cavity.
Eggs: White; 4 to 6 per clutch.
Song: Series of fluid twitters.
Other regions: NE, SE (coastal), PP (northern), PC, and SC.

OLIVE-SIDED FLYCATCHER

Like most members of its family, the olive-sided flycatcher eats mostly insects, many of which it takes on the wing. Honey bees and ants are particular favorites. The bird sometimes has been attracted to feeders where bits of meat and eggs, as well as live mealworms, are offered.

TREE SWALLOW

Because it includes bayberries as a major portion of its diet, the tree swallow is able to spend the winter months much farther north than other members of the swallow family. Although the bird also supplements its winter diet with various seeds, the best bet for attracting it are nesting boxes placed on poles in fields, especially if adjacent to ponds and lakes.

WILLOW FLYCATCHER

Gnats are the preferred food of the willow flycatcher, which generally gravitates toward areas that either are or resemble overgrown, abandoned orchards.

The willow flycatcher occupies much more open areas than most of its close relatives and, thus, comes into backyards within its range much more frequently and regularly. It eats mostly flying insects, supplemented with berries.

WILLOW FLYCATCHER
Empidonax traillii
Family: Tyrannidae
Description: 5 to 6"; brownish green with off-white throat.
Habitat: Thick, overgrown, wooded areas.
Range: Breeds throughout the U.S., except for the southern California and the southeastern quarter of the country.
Nest: Plant fibers woven into cup, in shrub or small sapling.
Eggs: Milky white spotted and blotched with brown, mostly at larger end; 3 to 4 per clutch.
Song: "Fitz-bew" (wheezingly).
Other regions: NE, PP, and PC (northern).

GRAY JAY

Also known as the camp robber for its habit of visiting campsites, cabins, and the like to steal and scavenge food, the gray jay is a favorite of outdoor lovers wherever it occurs. It will eat almost anything, and becomes quite tame in areas of frequent camping.

The seeds of coniferous trees are particularly attractive to the gray jay as a winter food. It often sticks these seeds together into small bundles, using its saliva as a glue, to be stored away for later use.

GRAY JAY

Perisoreus canadensis
Family: Corvidae
Description: 10 to 13"; gray above, off-white below, white forehead and throat, black back of neck and stripe through eye.
Habitat: Woodlands of primarily coniferous species.
Range: Alaska south as far as the central U.S. along the Pacific Coast and in the Rockies, also throughout most of Canada.
Nest: Twigs and bits of bark woven into cup lined with feathers, near the trunk of a conifer.
Eggs: Grayish green spotted with brown-green; 2 to 5 per clutch.
Song: "Whee-ah, chuck-chuck."
Other regions: PC (northern) and SC.

VEERY

Catharus fuscescens
Family: Turdidae
Description: 6½ to 7¼"; red-brown above with spotting on breast.
Habitat: Damp woodlands, particularly deciduous.
Range: Breeds from southern Canada and northernmost U.S. south through the Rockies and Appalachians; winters in South America.
Nest: Leaves, plant fibers, and moss loosely woven into cup on ground in thick vegetation or in shrub.
Eggs: Blue-green; 3 to 5 per clutch.
Song: Series of calls spiraling downward.
Call: "Whew."

VEERY

Within its range, the veery is generally found wherever deciduous woodlands occur in close proximity to weedy and grassy areas. This combination provides insects as well as shrubs or trees that provide fruit. Even where abundant the veery is difficult to spot, but it can be attracted into the open by mimicking the squeaking distress call of a bird.

SWAINSON'S THRUSH

Breeding in the far north or in forests on remote mountains and wintering far south of the U.S., Swainson's thrush is not all that common a sight for most North American bird-watchers, except during migration. At this time the birds cross and appear in backyards along their pancontinental route. However, this migration takes place rather quickly, often at rates of 200 miles per night.

The bird is an effective forager, taking a great variety of insects and fruit, on the ground, in the trees, and while in flight.

SWAINSON'S THRUSH

Catharus ustulatus
Family: Turdidae
Description: 6½ to 7¾"; green-brown above, spotted below, pinkish yellow eye ring and cheek.
Habitat: Coniferous woodlands.
Range: Breeds from Alaska and central Canada south through the Appalachians and Rockies and along the Pacific Coast; winters in South America.
Nest: Twigs, moss, lichen, leaves, and grass tightly woven into cup, in shrub or small tree in woodland.
Eggs: Light green-blue spotted and blotched with brown; 3 to 4 per clutch.
Song: Series of musical phrases, each of different pitch.
Call: "Chuck."
Other regions: NE, PC, and SC.

WILSON'S WARBLER
Wilsonia pusilla
Family: Parulidae
Description: 4½ to 5"; male is brownish green above and yellow below with black crown; female lacks black crown.
Habitat: Damp woodlands with plenty of thickets and bogs, particularly along streams.
Range: Breeds from Alaska and the southern two-thirds of Canada south along the Rockies and the Pacific Coast; winters from Mexico south through Central America.
Nest: Leaves, moss, and plant fibers in loose mass lined with hair and plant fibers, in thick weeds on ground.
Eggs: White spotted with reddish brown; 4 to 6 per clutch.
Song: Stacatto series of chirps.
Other regions: PC and SC.

WILSON'S WARBLER
The Wilson's warbler is prized by spring migration birdwatchers for its bright coloration. This lovely species is also distinguished by its penchant for activity and singing, especially relative to other migratory warblers.

Whether it is on its nesting grounds or in migration, this bird tends to feed by swiftly darting into the air to snatch flying insects. It also searches for insects on the ground, rooting persistently among leaf litter.

WESTERN TANAGER
The western tanager is a much less shy bird than the rest of its family, even when protecting its young in the nest and after fledging. Nevertheless, the bird tends to stay within the shelter of the forest, until fruits and berries ripen. Then, the western tanager moves into the open to feed in tangles of berry bushes and vines, and in orchards. In some locales, this habit brings the bird into conflict with fruit growers, although it also eats a great many harmful insects.

WESTERN TANAGER
Piranga ludoviciana
Family: Thraupidae
Description: 6 to 7"; male is bright yellow with red head and black wings, back, and tail, white wing bars; female is brownish green with faint wing bars.
Habitat: Woodlands of coniferous or mixed species, particularly oak and pine.
Range: Breeds from the southwestern quarter of Canada south through the western U.S.; winters in Mexico.
Nest: Twigs, grass, and pine needles loosely woven into flat cup, on branch of oak or pine tree.
Eggs: Light blue-green spotted darker; 3 to 4 per clutch.
Song: Warble; "pit-ick" (repeated again and again).
Other regions: PP (western), SW, PC, and SC (western half).

BLACK-HEADED GROSBEAK

The black-headed grosbeak is another common raider of campsites in the West, scavenging just about anything edible that it finds. The bird's natural diet is composed mostly of insects and fruit. Sunflower seeds is the prime attraction at feeders. It comes readily to the feeder, where it soon becomes quite tame.

LAZULI BUNTING

Until late summer, when the new generation has fully vacated the nesting area and grown nearly to adult size, the lazuli bunting population keeps mostly to the forests and thickets. But, as the birds prepare for their southern migration in October, they spread out over much larger areas to feast on the plentiful bounty of weed seeds and insects. It's these few months when backyard birdwatchers have the best chance to attract the species with niger seeds and oil-type sunflower seeds.

BLACK-HEADED GROSBEAK

Pheucticus melanocephalus
Family: Fringillidae
Description: 7 to 8"; male has black head, wings, and tail with scattered white patches, burnt orange breast, yellow-brown back with black streaks; female has white eyebrows, light pinkish yellow underside and streaked breast.
Habitat: Open woodlands of deciduous species, particularly near water.
Range: Breeds throughout the western half of the U.S. and in the southwestern corner of Canada; winters in Mexico.
Nest: Twigs in loose mass lined with plant fibers and leaves, on deciduous tree limb.
Eggs: Light green spotted with brown; 3 to 4 per clutch.
Song: Warble similar to robin but softer.
Call: "Tick" (sharply).
Other regions: PP (western), SW, PC, and SC (extreme west).

RED CROSSBILL

The only food of the red crossbill is the seed of coniferous trees, which remains available to the bird throughout the year. For this reason, the red crossbill is often the first bird to nest in any area that it frequents. Also, for this same reason, when the cone crop fails in the northern forests, large numbers can be expected in suburban and rural areas far to the south, where they are particularly frequent visitors in backyards with cone-bearing trees.

LAZULI BUNTING

Passerina amoena
Family: Fringillidae
Description: 5 to 5½"; male is bright blue with red-brown breast, white underside and white bars on wings; female is brown, lighter on the underside, with fainter wing bars.
Habitat: Dry, brushy areas and overgrown areas.
Range: Breeds from southwestern Canada south across the western half of the U.S. as far south as New Mexico; winters in Mexico.
Nest: Plant fibers and grass loosely woven into cup in shrub.
Eggs: Light blue; 3 to 4 per clutch.
Song: Series of warbled phrases, descending then ascending the scale.
Other regions: PP (western), PC, and SC (western).

RED CROSSBILL
Loxia curvirostra
Family: Fringillidae
Description: 5¼ to 6½"; male is brownish red; female is greenish gray; both have distinctive crossed bill.
Habitat: Woodlands of coniferous species; also, in winter, conifers in residential areas.
Range: Breeds from Alaska and central Canada south throughout the western U.S. and along the Appalachians in the East; winters in same area but also south to Gulf of Mexico.
Nest: Bits of bark, plant fibers, and grass woven into flat cup lined with moss and fine plant fibers, near tip of branch of conifer.
Eggs: Light blue-green spotted with brown and purple; 3 to 5 per clutch.
Song: "Chipa-chipa-chipa, chee-chee-chee-chee."
Other regions: NE, SE (Appalachians), PP (northern two-thirds), PC, and SC.

For other birds that might be sighted in backyards in the Rockies region, refer to the following species in other chapters of this book:
Chapter One: Pancontinental Birds: All.
Chapter Two: Northeast & Mid-Atlantic: American tree sparrow, brown creeper, red-breasted nuthatch, white-breasted nuthatch, black-capped chickadee.
Chapter Three: Southeast: Eastern kingbird, gray catbird.
Chapter Four: Plains & Prairies: Bobolink, red-eyed vireo.
Chapter Five: Southwest: American dipper, fox sparrow, hermit thrush, plain titmouse, green-tailed towhee, canyon wren.
Chapter Seven: Pacific Coast: Marsh wren, mountain bluebird, evening grosbeak, yellow-headed blackbird.
Chapter Eight: Southern Canada: American redstart.

7.
Pacific Coast

PURPLE MARTIN

The purple martin was one of the first North American bird species to attract special efforts by humans. Native Americans used hollow gourds and later the first European settlers to the continent built martin houses near fields to attract the insect-eating birds. Unaided, the purple martins established their colonies in snags that woodpeckers had worked over and left filled with holes.

These early efforts, and even the naturally occurring colony sites, didn't hold a candle to some modern means of aiding the bird. Large martin houses today sometimes attract more than 200 pairs of the birds into one colony.

WINTER WREN

The winter wren is one of the most difficult of songbirds to locate. It spends most of its life crawling, like a small rodent, among the lowest and most inaccessible tangles of thickets and hedgerows.

Much of the winter wren population moves south for the colder months, despite the bird's common name. Some races of the bird, however, are not nearly so migratory. These races tend to winter in the same locales where they spend the rest of the year, as far north as some Alaskan islands.

PURPLE MARTIN

Progne subis
Family: Hirundinidae
Description: 7 to 8½"; male is dark, metallic blue; female duller above and pale gray below.
Habitat: Open woodland, agricultural, and residential areas.
Range: Breeds from southern Canada south across the U.S. except in the Rockies; winters in South America.
Nest: Grass and plant fibers stuffed in cavity.
Eggs: White; 4 to 6 per clutch.
Song: Watery warble.
Call: "Tee-tee."
Other regions: NE, SE, PP, SW, SC.

WINTER WREN

Troglodytes troglodytes
Family: Troglodytidae
Description: 4 to 5"; shades of brown throughout with a noticeably paler eyebrow.
Habitat: Thickets in woodlands of coniferous species.
Range: Breeds from southern Canada south along the Appalachians in the northeastern U.S. and along the Pacific Coast in the western U.S.; winters in the southeastern U.S. and U.S. Pacific Coast.
Nest: Twigs, moss, and grass arranged into loose bundle with entrance on one side and lined with softer plant fibers, hidden in the roots of a fallen tree.
Eggs: White spotted with brown; 4 to 8 per clutch.
Song: "Wheedle-wheedle-wheedle."
Call: "Kit-kit."
Other regions: NE, SE, PP (eastern), SW, and SC.

MARSH WREN
Cistothorus palustris
Family: Troglodytidae
Description: 4½ to 5½"; brown above with black and white streaks along back, black crown, white eyebrow, off-white below.
Habitat: Marsh areas and along waterways.
Range: All U.S.
Nest: Cattail, sedge, and grass strips woven into cup between cattail and bulrush stems that have been lashed together, lined with softer plant fibers and feathers and with opening on side.
Eggs: Brown spotted with darker brown; 3 to 8 per clutch.
Song: Trill, followed by gurgle, followed by trill.
Other regions: NE, SE, PP, SW, and RM.

MARSH WREN

As its name implies, the marsh wren is found almost exclusively in and quite near wetlands or bodies of water. However, it is not shy about including nearby backyards in its territory.

The bird's presence is not difficult to detect, particularly during the spring, when the male builds many "dummy" nests before the return of females as part of its courtship ritual.

MOUNTAIN BLUEBIRD

In winter, small flocks of mountain bluebirds descend from their mountain homes to roam throughout grasslands and plains in search of insects. Fruit, too, is much sought after in this sparse time of the year.

The state bird of Idaho and Nevada, the mountain bluebird is a cavity nester and will at times set up housekeeping in manmade nesting boxes.

VARIED THRUSH

The varied thrush is almost exclusively a ground feeder, eating a great variety of insects and berries that it finds there. It prefers to keep under cover as much as possible while it feeds. Therefore, a backyard that offers thick hedgerows or dense thickets, particularly adjacent to large tracts of woodland, is a prime attraction.

VARIED THRUSH
Ixoreus naevius
Family: Turdidae
Description: 9 to 10"; male is dark gray above, orange over eyes and on wings, breast is streaked brownish orange, belly is white; female is paler.
Habitat: Moist woodlands, particularly near bodies of water.
Range: Alaska south along coast to northern California.
Nest: Strips of bark, leaves, mosses, and twigs woven into cup lined with softer leaves and grasses, on branch 10 to 20' above ground.
Eggs: Pale blue lightly spotted with shades of brown; 2 to 5 per clutch.
Song: Lengthy, wavering whistle followed by a moment of silence followed by another lengthy, wavering whistle.
Other regions: SC (westernmost).

MOUNTAIN BLUEBIRD
Sialia currucoides
Family: Turdidae
Description: 7"; male is sky blue above and lighter blue below, white rump; female duller with grayish tint.
Habitat: Mountain meadows, plains, grasslands.
Range: Alaska south through southwestern Canada and the western U.S.
Nest: Grass, moss, and other plant fibers, stuffed into cavity.
Eggs: Pale blue; 5 to 6 per clutch.
Song: Soft warble.
Call: "Chur-wee."
Other regions: RM, SW, and SC (western).

WRENTIT

Stream borders all along the Pacific Coast are home to mated-for-life pairs of wrentits. The pairs do everything together, from feasting on ripe berries to hunting for insects to roosting tight against one another.

The wrentit family—Chamaeidae—is the only bird family completely confined to North America. It is a one-species family, most closely related to the babbler family—Timaliidae—of birds in Europe, Asia, and Africa. It shows no close relationship to any other species of North American birds.

WATER PIPIT

Late fall and winter are the only time of the year when the water pipit is found away from its habitat on the northern tundra. But, during this period, large flocks roam the fields to the south. When threatened, an entire flock rockets into the air as one, spins about in the air, and drops back to roughly the same spot just vacated.

WRENTIT

Chamaea fasciata
Family: Chamaeidae
Description: 6 to 7"; grayish brown above, streaked red-brown below, white eyes.
Habitat: Brushy and grassy areas.
Range: West of the Sierras.
Nest: Grasses, plant fibers, and twigs woven into cup with spider silk, in shrub or small tree.
Eggs: Pale bluish green; 2 to 5 per clutch.
Song: "Pit, pit, pit, pit, tr-r-r-r-r-r-r."
Call: "Pee-ka, pee-ka."

WATER PIPIT

Anthus spinoletta
Family: Motacillidae
Description: 6 to 7"; brown above creamy brown with streaking below white at outer edges of tail feathers.
Habitat: Tundra, beach, barren, a agricultural areas.
Range: Breeds from Alaska south along the Pacific Coast south halfwa into U.S., also in northern Canada; winters from the southern U.S. south through Central America.
Nest: Grass and twigs woven into cup at rock or tuft of weeds.
Eggs: Gray spotted with brown and scrawled with black; 3 to 5 per clute
Song: Series of trills.
Calls: "Pip-pip."
Other regions: SE, PP (southern), SW, and SC (extreme west).

WHITE-CROWNED SPARROW

Much of what we know about the physical aspects of bird migration is a result of laboratory work involving the white-crowned sparrow.

This common bird has been known to come quite close to an observer who makes a high-pitched, squeaking noise.

On their breeding grounds, several dozen white-crowned sparrows can often be heard singing simultaneously. This activity is not restricted to the male, although it does continue to sing—generally throughout the entire day—for a longer, sustained period, while the female is occupied on the nest incubating the eggs.

WHITE-CROWNED SPARROW

Zonotrichia leucophrys
Family: Fringillidae
Description: 6 to 7½"; streaked brown above, black-and-white-striped crown, gray below, pink bill.
Habitat: Thick brush near open grassy areas.
Range: Breeds from Alaska and northern Canada south in the West to the southwestern U.S.; winters from Pennsylvania south in the eastern U.S., Oklahoma south in the middle of the country and throughout the U.S. West.
Nest: Twigs and grass loosely woven into cup lined with softer grass and hair, on or close to the ground.
Eggs: Green spotted with brown; 3 to 6 per clutch.

99

YELLOW-HEADED BLACKBIRD

Availability of fresh water is an absolute must for the marsh-loving yellow-headed blackbird. For nesting, colonies of the bird prefer to be completely surrounded by water. But at other times, properties that border these habitats also attract use by the yellow-headed blackbird.

This is the signature bird of slough-type environments, where it occurs in fairly large flocks in its range. When encountered under such conditions, the chatter of the birds drowns out nearly all other sounds.

EVENING GROSBEAK

Before backyard bird-feeding became the popular pastime it is today, the evening grosbeak was mostly restricted to the western half of the U.S. With the incredible boom in birdfeeders, however, this species has found the food supply to enable it to spend the winters months farther north and east. Today the evening grosbeak breeds all the way to the Atlantic coast.

It remains a feeder bird, with large flocks frequenting all feeders throughout their territories and devouring incredible amounts of seed. Oil-type sunflower seeds are a favorite.

YELLOW-HEADED BLACKBIRD

Xanthocephalus xanthocephalus
Family: Icteridae
Description: 8 to 11"; male has lemon yellow head, neck, and breast and is black everywhere else, except for white marks on wings; female is duller and smaller.
Habitat: Marshy, swampy areas near fresh water.
Range: Western U.S. and Canada.
Nest: Plant stems and fibers woven into loose basket between marsh-weed stems.
Eggs: White spotted with brown; 3 to 5 per clutch.
Song: "Oka-wee-wee."
Other regions: PP (western), SW, RM, and SC (western).

EVENING GROSBEAK

Coccothraustes vespertinus
Family: Fringillidae
Description: 7½ to 8½"; male is yellow on face, lower back, rump, and underside with a brown head, white patches on the wings, and a greenish yellow bill; female is duller with a gray tint.
Habitat: Woodlands and suburban areas.
Range: Breeds from southern Canada south through the U.S. West; winters south to southern California and Texas in the West and South Carolina in the East.
Nest: Twigs arranged in loose cup lined with plant fibers, in coniferous tree.
Eggs: Bluish green spotted with brown, gray, and olive; 3 to 5 per clutch.
Song: Series of quick whistles.
Call: "Peet, peet, creek."
Other regions: NE, PP (northern), RM, SW, and SC.

For other birds that might be sighted in backyards in the Pacific Coast region, refer to the following species in other chapters of the book:
Chapter One: Pancontinental Birds: All.
Chapter Two: Northeast & Mid-Atlantic: Northern cardinal, white-throated sparrow, American tree sparrow, purple finch, brown creeper, red-breasted nuthatch, white-breasted nuthatch, black-capped chickadee.
Chapter Three: Southeast: Blue-gray gnatcatcher.
Chapter Six: Rockies: Gray jay, lazuli bunting, red crossbill, black-headed grosbeak, willow flycatcher, tree swallow, Swainson's thrush, western tanager, Wilson's warbler.

8.
Southern Canada

WOOD THRUSH

Hylocichla mustelina
Family: Turdidae
Description: 7½ to 8½"; brown above, reddish on head, white below spotted with black.
Habitat: Deciduous woodlands with heavy undergrowth.
Range: Breeds from southeastern Canada south through the eastern half of the U.S. as far as northern Florida; winters from Mexico south to Panama.
Nest: Twigs, grass, and mud formed into cup lined with fine grass, in a small tree or shrub.
Eggs: Greenish blue; 3 to 5 per clutch.
Song: Series of flutelike notes ending in swift trill.
Call: "Pip, pip, pip."
Other regions: NE, SE, and PP (eastern).

NORTHERN PARULA WARBLER

Parula americana
Family: Parulidae
Description: 4 to 5"; blue above, yellowish green on back, yellow throat and breast, white underside, two white bars on each wing.
Habitat: Moist woodlands, particularly near water.
Range: Breeds from southeastern Canada south throughout the eastern U.S.; winters from Mexico south to South America and in the Caribbean.
Nest: Grass and other plant fibers woven into basket, hidden in beard moss.
Eggs: White spotted with brown; 3 to 6 per clutch.
Song: "Sweet-sweet-sweet, little-more-sweet."
Call: "Bzzzzz-zip."
Other regions: NE, SE, and PP (eastern).

WOOD THRUSH

The wood thrush is mostly a species of damp woodlands, but it has adapted well to the changing landscape. Today the bird is not an uncommon sight in city parks and suburban backyards.

A wide variety of insects form the bulk of the wood thrush's diet, but many of our berry-producing shrubs and vines, as well as many wild weed species that invade our backyards, also attract the bird.

NORTHERN PARULA WARBLER

In the northern extent of its range, the northern parula warbler can only be found where there is beard moss, with which the bird hides its basketlike nest. During migration, however, the species frequents all types of deciduous trees in a range of habitats.

A large majority of the bird's diet is made up of insects, regardless of season or location.

CHESTNUT-SIDED WARBLER

Dendroica pensylvanica
Family: Parulidae
Description: 4½ to 5½"; black streaked back, white underside, yellowish green crown and back, red-brown line on each side.
Habitat: Open woodland and brushland.
Range: Breeds from southern Canada south through the eastern U.S., farther in the Appalachians: winters in Central America.
Nest: Grass and plant fibers arranged in loose mass lined with hair and finer plant fibers, in small tree or shrub close to ground.
Eggs: White spotted with brown; 3 to 5 per clutch.
Song: "Very, very, very, very, pleased, to-meet-ya."
Other regions: NE and SE (Appalachians).

CHESTNUT-SIDED WARBLER

The chestnut-sided warbler is another of the songbird species that have undergone something of a population boom as abandoned farmlands throughout its range have grown back into dense areas of shrubs and thickets.

Backyards near and adjacent to those locations stand a good chance of attracting the birds.

BLACK-THROATED BLUE WARBLER

One of the least skittish members of the warbler family, the black-throated blue warbler often will allow a slowly and carefully moving observer to get to within a few feet of it without taking flight.

It also is one of the most common migrants through the eastern half of the U.S., where it readily takes seeds and fruits offered at backyard feeders.

BLACK-THROATED BLUE WARBLER

Dendroica caerulescens
Family: Parulidae
Description: 4½ to 5½"; male is bluish gray above, off-white below, with a black face, throat, and sides; female greenish brown with white eyebrow and wing patches.
Habitat: Woodlands of mixed deciduous and coniferous.
Range: Breeds from southeastern Canada south through the northeastern U.S. as far south as Georgia in the Appalachians; winters in Gulf of Mexico.
Nest: Grass and leaves collected in loose mass lined with spider silk and hair, in small tree or shrub close to ground.
Eggs: White spotted with brown; 3 to 5 per clutch.
Song: "Zee, zee, zee, zoo, zee."
Call: "Trees, trees."
Other regions: NE and SE (Appalachians).

BLACKPOLL WARBLER

Dendroica striata
Family: Parulidae
Description: 5 to 6"; male streaked with gray and brown above, black on sides, white below and on sides of face, black cap; female greenish with streaks.
Habitat: Coniferous woodlands.
Range: Breeds from Alaska and northern Canada south through southern Canada; winters in South America.
Nest: Twigs and plant fibers arrange in loose collection lined with feathers, in small coniferous tree.
Eggs: White spotted with brown; 3 to 5 per clutch.
Song: "Seet-seet-seet-seet-seet-seet-seet-seet."

BLACKPOLL WARBLER

The blackpoll warbler is one of the most abundant warblers in the eastern half of the continent. Birdwatchers willing to invest long periods of time in watching their spring and fall migrations have logged hundreds of the birds in a single day. This migration usually comes later in the spring than that of most warbler species.

Its northward movement is rather leisurely across the U.S., taking from twenty-five days to a month to advance from the southern to the northern border—a distance of about one thousand miles. When it passes into more northern areas of its range, where the spring comes more gradually, the bird increases its speed and covers the remaining two thousand or more miles in less than two weeks.

AMERICAN REDSTART

The American redstart is one of the most abundant songbirds in North America because the continent currently is covered with its preferred type of habitat—second-growth woodlands, the growth that follows logging and other clear-cutting operations.

The species eats mostly insects native to its forest haunts, supplemented with some fruits, notably those of the barberry, a popular backyard hedge species.

CONNECTICUT WARBLER

The Connecticut warbler is only an infrequent migrant to the state for which it is named and where it was discovered in 1812 by Alexander Wilson. It is much more common to the north and is always shy and elusive. Wetlands are key to the bird's presence in eastern areas, although it primarily occupies dry woodland ridges in the western part of its range, where it is more numerous.

AMERICAN REDSTART
Setophaga ruticilla
Family: Parulidae
Description: 4½ to 5½"; male is black with bright orange on wings and tail, white belly; female replaces the male's black with olive brown and the male's orange with yellow.
Habitat: Second-growth deciduous woodlands, thickets.
Range: Breeds from central Canada south throughout the eastern U.S. (except for the Deep South) and along the Rockies; winters in South America.
Nest: Grass, twigs, plant fibers, and spider silk woven into cup and lined with grass and hair, in a small tree.
Eggs: White spotted with brown; 3 to 5 per clutch.
Song: "Tzee-tzee-tzee-tzee-ah."
Other regions: NE, SE (not Deep South), PP (eastern), and RM.

CONNECTICUT WARBLER
Oporornis agilis
Family: Parulidae
Description: 4½ to 5½"; greenish brown above, yellow below, gray on head, throat, and upper breast, white eye ring.
Habitat: Coniferous woodlands.
Range: Breeds throughout south-central Canada; winters in northern South America.
Nest: Loose collection of grass hidden in undergrowth, often in moss.
Eggs: Off-white blotched with brown; 3 to 5 per clutch.
Song: "Beecher-beecher-beecher-beecher."

SCARLET TANAGER
Piranga olivacea
Family: Thraupidae
Description: 7 to 8"; male bright red with black wings and tail; female brownish green.
Habitat: Woodlands, particularly pine and oak.
Range: Breeds from southeastern Canada south through the eastern U.S. to the central region of the country; winters in South America.
Nest: Twigs and plant stems arranged in loose mass lined with grasses, in tree.
Eggs: Green spotted with brown; 2 to 4 per clutch.
Song: Burry version of American robin's song.
Call: "Chick-burr."
Other regions: NE and PP (extreme east).

ROSE-BREASTED GROSBEAK
Pheucticus ludovicianus
Family: Fringillidae
Description: 7½ to 8½"; male is black and white with red patch on breast; female is streaked brown and white throughout with a white eyebrow.
Habitat: Moist woodlands near areas of mixed shrubs and grasslands.
Range: Breeds from southern Canada south through the central U.S.; winters from Mexico south to South America.
Nest: Twigs and grass woven into loose cup, in tree not far above ground.
Eggs: Purple spotted with off-white; 3 to 6 eggs per clutch.
Song: Whistled, robinlike phrases.
Call: "Chink."
Other regions: NE, SE (Appalachians), and PP (northeast).

SCARLET TANAGER

The scarlet tanager is one of the most brilliantly colored North American birds. It also is one of the most reclusive, spending a great deal of time among the treetops. A welcome sight for anyone with trees on their property, the scarlet tanager is nearly unequaled in its abilities to locate and capture all manner of insects, even the most well-camouflaged moths and caterpillars. Despite its hermit tendencies, the scarlet tanager is not adverse to close contact with humans—especially when they inadvertently assist the bird in locating insects with their farm equipment. In springtime, this determined species has been known to follow farmers' plows to pluck earthworms and grubs in their wake.

ROSE-BREASTED GROSBEAK

The rose-breasted grosbeak is primarily a seed eater, particularly the seeds of many species of deciduous trees. It forages among the branches of these trees for the seeds, as well as the blossoms and buds. The bird also takes many insects and some grains and fruit.

Like most finch species, the rose-breasted grosbeak is an active feeder visitor, generally appearing in small flocks.

RUSTY BLACKBIRD

Wooded swamps and moist woodlands are the preferred habitat of the rusty blackbird, where the birds are generally seen in small flocks working their way through the leaf litter in search of food.

For most backyard birdwatchers, the rusty blackbird is a migratory visitor. However, its arrival is spectacular, both for the large flocks in which it travels and for the incredible noise the birds produce. In many regions, the rusty blackbird takes on the robin's traditional role as harbinger of spring.

RUSTY BLACKBIRD

Euphagus carolinus
Family: Icteridae
Description: 8 to 9"; bluish or greenish tint over black, taking on a rusty tint in fall, especially about the head, back, and breast.
Habitat: Swampy areas and moist woodlands.
Range: Breeds from Alaska and northern Canada south through southern Canada; winters throughout the eastern half of the U.S.
Nest: Twigs arranged in bulky mass lined with grass and moss, in small tree or shrub near or over water.
Eggs: Bluish green blotched with brown; 3 to 6 per clutch.
Song: "Chak, chak, chak, kiss-lay."
Other regions: NE, SE, and PP (eastern).

For other birds that might be sighted in backyards in the Southern Canada region, refer to the following species in other chapters of the book:

Chapter One: Pancontinental Birds: All.

Chapter Two: Northeast & Mid-Atlantic: Blue jay, northern cardinal, white-throated sparrow, purple finch, pine warbler, eastern bluebird, brown creeper, red-breasted nuthatch, white-breasted nuthatch, black-capped chickadee.

Chapter Three: Southeast: Eastern phoebe, eastern kingbird, eastern wood pewee, great crested flycatcher, blue-gray gnatcatcher, gray catbird, black-and-white warbler, eastern meadowlark.

Chapter Four: Plains & Prairies: Bobolink, indigo bunting, ovenbird, red-eyed vireo.

Chapter Five: Southwest: American dipper, Say's phoebe, fox sparrow, hermit thrush, plain titmouse, green-tailed towhee.

Chapter Six: Rockies: Gray jay, lazuli bunting, red crossbill, black-headed grosbeak, tree swallow, Swainson's thrush, western tanager, Wilson's warbler.

Chapter Seven: Pacific Coast: Winter wren, mountain bluebird, evening grosbeak, yellow-headed blackbird, water pipit, purple martin.

APPENDIX: FOOD PREFERENCES

Cracked corn: mourning dove, horned lark, chipping sparrow, song sparrow, red-winged blackbird, blue jay, white-throated sparrow, indigo bunting, dickcissel, lark bunting, Henslow's sparrow, pyrrhuloxia, gray jay, black-headed grosbeak, rusty blackbird.

Corn kernels (whole): American crow, blue jay, gray jay, rusty blackbird.

Fruit, fruit bits, berries: American robin, northern mockingbird, cedar waxwing, vesper sparrow, northern oriole, house finch, pine warbler, eastern phoebe, gray catbird, brown thrasher, painted bunting, orchard oriole, cactus wren, ruby-crowned kinglet, hermit thrush, green-tailed towhee, fox sparrow, gray jay, western tanager, lazuli bunting, wrentit, white-crowned sparrow, American redstart, scarlet tanager.

Insects (not much of a feeder bird): house wren, loggerhead shrike, warbling vireo, yellow warbler, common yellowthroat, yellow-breasted chat, brown creeper, eastern bluebird, pine warbler, tree swallow, eastern wood pewee, eastern phoebe, great crested flycatcher, eastern kingbird, blue-gray gnatcatcher, black-and-white warbler, Kentucky warbler, painted bunting, eastern meadowlark, vermilion flycatcher, red-eyed vireo, prothonotary warbler, ovenbird, Louisiana waterthrush, bobolink, orchard oriole, Say's phoebe, canyon wren, American dipper, ruby-crowned kinglet, hermit thrush, Bell's vireo, summer tanager, olive-sided flycatcher, willow flycatcher, tree swallow, veery, Swainson's thrush, Wilson's warbler, purple martin, winter, wren, marsh wren, mountain bluebird, varied thrush, water pipit, wood thrush, northern parula warbler, chestnut-sided warbler, black-throated blue warbler, blackpoll warbler, Connecticut warbler.

Millet: mourning dove, song sparrow, red-winged blackbird, house finch, pine siskin, white-throated sparrow, Henslow's sparrow, fox sparrow, gray jay, Swainson's thrush, white-crowned sparrow, yellow-headed blackbird, rusty blackbird.

Niger seed: house finch, pine siskin, American goldfinch, lark bunting, green-tailed towhee, lazuli bunting, red crossbill.

Nut meats: dark-eyed junco, northern oriole, blue jay, tufted titmouse, red-breasted nuthatch, white-throated sparrow, brown thrasher, gray jay, rusty blackbird.

Oil-type sunflower seed: mourning dove, horned lark, chipping sparrow, song sparrow, dark-eyed junco, house finch, pine siskin, American goldfinch, blue jay, black-capped chickadee, tufted titmouse, red-breasted nuthatch, northern cardinal, white-throated sparrow, purple finch, Carolina chickadee, dickcissel, lark bunting, Henslow's sparrow, plain titmouse, pyrrhuloxia, green-tailed towhee, fox sparrow, gray jay, Swainson's thrush, black-headed grosbeak, lazuli bunting, red crossbill, yellow-headed blackbird, evening grosbeak, American redstart, rose-breasted grosbeak, rusty blackbird.

Peanut butter: northern mockingbird, song sparrow, dark-eyed junco, tufted titmouse, plain titmouse, gray jay, black-capped chickadee.

Suet: northern mockingbird, rufous-sided towhee, chipping sparrow, song sparrow, dark-eyed junco, red-winged blackbird, northern oriole, blue jay, tufted titmouse, red-breasted nuthatch, brown creeper, plain titmouse, gray jay, black-capped chickadee.

Table scraps: American crow, blue jay, gray jay, rusty blackbird, European starling, English house sparrow.

50 ADDITIONAL NORTH AMERICAN BIRDS

CANADA GOOSE
Branta canadensis
Regions: all.
Habitat: wide variety of habitats near water, agricultural fields.

WOOD DUCK
Aix sponsa
Regions: NE, SE, PP, PC.
Habitat: all sorts of inland waters, generally in forested areas.

MALLARD
Anas platyrhynchos
Regions: all.
Habitat: bodies of water, generally shallow.

RED-TAILED HAWK
Buteo jamaicensis
Regions: all.
Habitat: fields, brushy areas with scattered trees.

AMERICAN KESTREL
Flaco sparverius
Regions: all.
Habitat: fields, brushy areas, residential areas, with scattered trees.

RING-NECKED PHEASANT
Phasianus colchicus
Regions: NE, PP, SC (western).
Habitat: agricultural areas, waste areas, suburban areas, woodland edges.

NORTHERN BOBWHITE
Colinus virginianus
Regions: NE, SE, PP (eastern).
Habitat: bushy, grassy areas, agricultural lands.

CALIFORNIA QUAIL
Callipepla californica
Regions: PC, SW (western), RM (western).
Habitat: brushy, grassy, and weedy areas; agricultural lands, woodland edges.

KILLDEER
Charadrius vociferus
Regions: all.
Habitat: agricultural areas, shorelines, meadows.

ROCK DOVE, ALSO KNOWN AS COMMON PIGEON
Columba livia
Regions: all.
Habitat: generally near human habitation, especially in cities and around barnyards.

COMMON GROUND DOVE
Columbia passerina
Regions: SE, PP (southern), SW (southern).
Habitat: open, grassy, and weedy areas; agricultural lands.

COMMON BARN OWL
Tyto alba
Regions: all U.S.
Habitat: open grassy and weedy areas, often near human habitation; agricultural lands.

EASTERN SCREECH OWL
Otus asio
Regions: NE, SE, PP, SC (eastern).
Habitat: open woodlands, parks, residential areas.

GREAT HORNED OWL
Bubo virginianus
Regions: all.
Habitat: wide variety of forested habitats, including residential and park areas.

WHIP-POOR-WILL
Caprimulgus vociferus
Regions: NE, SE, PP (eastern), SW, PC, SC (southeastern).
Habitat: open woodland, woodland edges.

CHIMNEY SWIFT
Chaetura pelagica
Regions: NE, SE, PP, SC (eastern).
Habitat: open areas, particularly near human habitation.

RUBY-THROATED HUMMINGBIRD
Archilochus colubris
Regions: NE, SE, PP (eastern), SC (eastern half).
Habitat: wooded areas, including parks; residential areas, agricultural lands.

BLACK-CHINNED HUMMINGBIRD
Archilochus alexandri
Regions: PP (southern), SW, RM, PC (northern), SC (western).
Habitat: open woodland, along wooded waterways, parks, residential areas, chaparral areas.

ANNA'S HUMMINGBIRD
Calypte anna
Regions: SW, PC, SC (extreme west).
Habitat: open woodland, grassland, or scrubland; residential areas

RED-HEADED WOODPECKER
Melanerpes erythrocephalus
Regions: NE, SE, PP, SC (eastern).
Habitat: open deciduous woodland, parks, residential areas with trees.

RED-BELLIED WOODPECKER
Melanerpes carolinus
Regions: NE, SE, PP (eastern).
Habitat: open deciduous woodland, parks, residential areas with trees, swamps.

DOWNY WOODPECKER
Picoides pubescens
Regions: all.
Habitat: deciduous woodland, parks, residential areas with trees, wood-lined waterways.

HAIRY WOODPECKER
Picoides villosus
Regions: all.
Habitat: open woodland, parks, residential areas with significant numbers of trees.

YELLOW-BELLIED SAPSUCKER
Sphyrapicus varius
Regions: NE, SE, PP (eastern), SC.
Habitat: Open deciduous or mixed woodlands.

NORTHERN FLICKER
Colaptes auratus
Regions: all.
Habitat: open woodland, parks, residential areas with scattered groups of trees and undergrowth.

LEAST FLYCATCHER
Empidonax minimus
Regions: NE, PP (northern), SC.
Habitat: open woodland and edges, brushy areas, parks, residential areas.

VIOLET-GREEN SWALLOW
Tachycineta thalassina
Regions: RM, SW, PC, SC (western).
Habitat: open woodland, agricultural areas, along waterways.

CLIFF SWALLOW
Hirundo pyrrhonota
Regions: NE, PP, SW, RM, PC, SC.
Habitat: open areas near waterways.

BARN SWALLOW
Hirundo rustica
Regions: all, but most southern U.S.
Habitat: open areas near waterways.

SCRUB JAY
Aphelocoma coerulescens
Regions: RM, PC, SC.
Habitat: Scrublands, brushy areas, parks, residential areas, woodlands.

BLACK-BILLED MAGPIE
Pica pica
Regions: PP (western), RM, SC (western).
Habitat: grassy areas, scrubland, woodland areas, agricultural areas, residential areas, all with scattered trees and shrubs.

BUSHTIT
Psaltriparus minimus
Regions: PP, SW, RM, PC, SC (western).
Habitat: woodlands, scrublands, chaparral areas, residential areas with scattered brushy areas.

CAROLINA WREN
Thryothorus ludovicianus
Regions: NE, SE, PP, (southeastern).
Habitat: deciduous woodland, parks, residential areas with trees.

GOLDEN-CROWNED KINGLET
Regulus satrapa
Regions: all.
Habitat: coniferous woodland, scrubland.

WESTERN BLUEBIRD
Sialia mexicana
Regions: PP (western), SE, RM (southern), PC, SC (western).
Habitat: open woodland, woodland along waterways.

EUROPEAN STARLING
Sturnus vulgaris
Regions: NE, SE, PP.
Habitat: woodland, agricultural areas, residential areas.

WHITE-EYED VIREO
Viero griseus
Regions: NE, SE, PP (eastern).
Habitat: scrubland, brushy areas.

ORANGE-CROWNED WARBLER
Vermivora celata
Regions: SE, RM, SW, PC, SC.
Habitat: woodland, chaparall, wood-lined waterways, woodland edges.

YELLOW-RUMPED WARBLER
Dendroica coronata
Regions: NE, SE, PP (southern), SW, RM, PC, SC.
Habitat: open woodland, parks, residential areas with trees.

BLUE GROSBEAK
Guiraca caerulea
Regions: NE (southern), SE, PP, (southern), SW, RM (southern).
Habitat: open woodland, weedy areas with scattered shrubs and trees.

BROWN TOWHEE
Pipilo fuscus
Regions: PP (southwestern), SW, PC.
Habitat: scrubland near water, woodland.

FIELD SPARROW
Spizella pusilla
Regions: NE, SE, PP.
Habitat: reverting agricultural areas, woodland edges, residential areas with trees and shrubs.

SAVANNAH SPARROW
Passerculus sandwichensis
Regions: all.
Habitat: open grasslands, agricultural areas.

GRASSHOPPER SPARROW
Ammodramus savannarum
Regions: SE, PP, SW.
Habitat: reverting agricultural areas, grassy areas.

BREWER'S BLACKBIRD
Euphagus cyanocephalus
Regions: SE, PP (southern), SW, RM, PC, SC (western).
Habitat: woodland, woodland along waterways, shrubland, agricultural areas.

BOAT-TAILED GRACKLE
Quiscalus major
Regions: NE (coastal), SE (coastal).
Habitat: agricultural areas, marshland in coastal areas.

COMMON GRACKLE
Quiscalus quiscula
Regions: NE, SE, PP, SC (eastern two-thirds).
Habitat: open woodland, woodland edges, agricultural areas, residential areas.

BROWN-HEADED COWBIRD
Molothrus ater
Regions: all.
Habitat: woodland, woodland edges, agricultural areas, residential areas.

SCOTT'S ORIOLE
Icterus parisorum
Regions: PP (southwestern), SW, PC (southern).
Habitat: scrubland.

COMMON REDPOLL
Carduelis flammea
Regions: NE (northern), SC.
Habitat: woodland, scrubland, agricultural areas.

PHOTO CREDITS